T0118357

Large Circles and Bold Lines

Large Circles and Bold Lines

A Quaker Scientist's Meditation on the Subject of Meaning in His Life

Stan Cherim

iUniverse, Inc.
Bloomington

Large Circles and Bold Lines
A Quaker Scientist's Meditation on the Subject of Meaning in His Life

iUniverse books may be ordered through booksellers or by contacting:

iUniverse
1663 Liberty Drive
Bloomington, IN 47403
www.iuniverse.com
1-800-Authors (1-800-288-4677)

ISBN: 978-1-4620-2013-3 (pbk)
ISBN: 978-1-4620-2014-0 (ebk)

Printed in the United States of America

iUniverse rev. date: 05/06/2011

CONTENTS

Introduction

Large Circles and Bold Lines is an ongoing journal about a Quaker scientist's search for meaning in his life. These protracted essays are, in the context of my search, tentative and in a state of flux. They have come out of my conviction that there can be, and ought to be, a symbiotic relationship between science and religion. Both realms of human activity tend to ask these similar questions: How did we get here and evolve into the species we have become? Is there some purpose to our creation and in the years of our life? And, on the uniquely personal level, what is the meaning of it all? Any attempt on my part to answer questions like these would be stunningly pretentious, and I won't go there. Instead, my aim is to raise more questions that can emerge from a positive and constructive synthesis of science and religion—Quakerism in particular. There are a few bits and pieces in my writing that may look like answers, but they are more likely to be an expression of my attitudes toward human value systems and what is popularly called "conventional wisdom." At this point it may be useful to separate this introduction into scientific and Quaker parts.

The Science Part

"(Physicists) wonder what the universe is really made of, how it works, what we are doing in it, and where it is going . . . . In short, they do the same thing that we (non-scientists) do on starry nights when we look up at the vastness of the universe and feel overwhelmed by it, and part of it at the same time. That is what physicists do and the clever rascals get paid for doing it."

I love this quotation. It was written by a sociologist, Gary Zukav, in his New Age physics book, *The Dancing Wu Li Masters.* Zukav offers the kind of wit and whimsy that can be found in the *Tao of Pooh* and other similar, not-so-heavy philosophical tomes. But he hit the nail on the head. It is all about human curiosity and our capacity for astonishment. It's why I became a scientist.In the next essay, dealing with the question of physical reality, I've cited a number of relevant quotations attributed to some of the world's prominent scientists. Proper citation is absolutely essential, but that alone is frustrating because there are so many fascinating stories about these scientists. Biographical details reveal their very human nature—adventures, discoveries, and personal anecdotes that can make us weep or smile. Therefore, in an effort to pay homage to these people in a way that a standard bibliography, loaded with a scholarly looking bunch of "ibids." and "op. cits." can't possibly do, I have an alternative suggestion. With an obvious lack of modesty, I'll rate my plan as twenty-first century brilliant. It is simply a wonderful spinoff of our computer world that gives us access to the lives and accomplishments of great people if we just Google their name. The Wikipedia (No, not Wikileaks!) website, even with its sometimes dubious accuracy, is a great place to start.

The choices among the variety of scientific disciplines can be difficult, and it often turns out to be a combination. For me it was the dual influence of my little chemistry set in the basement when I was very young, followed later by the joyful experience of having a wonderful biology teacher in high school. So, I eventually became a biochemist way back in the ancient decade of the 1960s. I can still recall, with a shudder of disbelief, how different life was in the research laboratories in those days. Oh, there was a lot of good science going on, but our lack of concern for safety and proper procedure was sometimes a bit hair-raising. Nobody cared about wearing protective goggles or filling pipettes (graduated glass straws) by mouth instead of with rubber bulbs. A necktie, which most of us wore in those days, was always good for wiping the tip of a pipette—corrosive liquid droplets notwithstanding. Fume hoods to exhaust noxious gases were hit or miss, and it didn't matter that much since a lot of us were pipe smokers anyway. We tried so hard to look suave and professorial! We used to kid ourselves by telling each other that the accidental dropping of pipe ashes into an experiment could only yield good results. My research years at the University of Pennsylvania were always intellectually stimulating, and I still remember some of the dynamic seminars presented by outstanding scientists.

But research gave way to teaching when I finally became convinced that interacting with students in the classroom was what I really loved. It suited my temperament; it spoke to my condition.

During a teenage period of rebellion against authority, and with a smug belief that science could provide, or would eventually provide, the answers to any questions about meaning and purpose, academic learning and laboratory experience progressed. My certainty about the omnipotence of science, however, started to crumble. It had a lot to do with not being able to find the answers that science was supposed to reveal. It had more to do with a rediscovered appreciation for the miracle of life. I was increasingly overwhelmed by the beauty and complexity of life in the broadest sense, and there was the growing awareness deep within me that it was unlikely that life could have evolved accidentally as a result of some pointless cosmic happening. The cold, dispassionate facade that I once assumed to be *de rigueur* for a scientist gave way to a foolishly suppressed sentimentality that caused me real unhappiness whenever I had to sacrifice animals for my research. Various forays into the world of biochemical research made it necessary for me to sacrifice frogs, mice, rats, and pigeons. The slaughterhouse near the university at least made it easy to get the beef hearts I used in mitochondrial research. With a few mental gymnastics, letting someone else do the killing for me seemed to work. But there was an ever present feeling of sacredness involved that I found stressful. There is little doubt that the use of animals in research is essential in the conquest of human disorders, but it was an inability to cope well with animal sacrifice that propelled my move toward physical chemistry. Electronic instruments don't suffer and bleed, and that's much better for the softhearted like me. I do not align myself with the antivivisectionists; I do respect their right to believe as they do. I do not concur, however, with radical extremist actions of any stripe. Violent activity by those who arrogantly claim to know and to do God's command is something I totally reject. We all know about the outrageous crimes committed by radical pro-life fanatics in their war against abortion for any reason, but the sad part is how counterproductive they are in finding the common ground where pro-life and pro-choice people can work together. There is much more about the role of science in the search for meaning in the essay dealing with the question of physical reality. A brief discussion of the Quaker part of this introduction follows.

The Quaker Part

While there's nothing mysterious about claiming science as a profession, the characteristics of a Quaker may require a little clarification. Firstly, I want to make it crystal clear that we are not Amish, Puritans, Shakers, or the like. They may be lovely people, but they are not remotely related to us—especially the Shakers, who demanded celibacy. They are obviously long gone. And in this day and age you won't find Quakers who look like that funny old guy pictured on boxes of Quaker Oats. Let me try to explain who we are by putting together a few thumbnail sketches of our beliefs and practices—with absolutely no desire to proselytize. We don't do that. If anyone is curious enough to learn more, we have a book of *Faith and Practice* that you can probably find in any library.Historically, we were regarded as an extremely heretical defection from the Church of England (Anglican) because of a great deal of discontent about the way the church was being run. I'll spare you the details. There were enough issues to make up a list that would leave you glassy-eyed. Anyway, there was an Englishman named George Fox who was the principle founder of our sect about four hundred years ago. It wasn't the intent of our early leaders to form a new denomination; their original goal was to bring about a reformation of the church in order to do away with what they believed to be unacceptable hypocrisy and corruption. The Religious Society of Friends, more commonly known as Quakers, might be properly described in today's computer terminology as "default" Christian. Many of our members insist that they are Christian in the mainstream sense of the word, but many others believe they are something other than that as defined in terms of standard Protestant theology. Some Quakers are unitarian, ethicist, agnostic, social activist, Jewish Quakers, Catholic Quakers, and so on. The fact is, there is no single creedal statement that all Quakers must subscribe to. The freedom that Quakers have in the development of their own personal belief system is something we cherish. If they choose to believe that God *is* love, universal intelligence, a monarch of some sort, Jesus, Allah, or whatever, that is up to them, and their right to believe as they do is totally respected.

We usually gather in a rather architecturally plain building on a Sunday morning for what we call a meeting for worship. You're not likely to find stained glass, pulpits, steeples, pews, and the like unless you're at a rural pastoral meeting in the Midwest. Pastoral meetings are hardly distinguishable from your typical Protestant churches. They do identify with Quaker principles while tending to be more evangelical. Our testimony in support of simplicity is vigorous, as it applies to all aspects of our way of life. Attendees settle into a period of silent worship, alternately described as meditation or contemplation—almost like a page out of Zen Buddhism protocol. There is usually no hymn singing, responsive readings, or liturgical order in the "services." We have a Friends' Hymnal, but the hymn singing more likely takes place before or after the silent worship. There is no priest or minister in charge. The person closest to that role is called the clerk. It is his or her job to signal the end of the period of silent worship by the ritual shaking of hands with whomever is nearby on a bench at the front of the meeting room. It is appropriately called the "facing bench," but there is no special status assigned to it. Once upon a time it was the place for prominent elder members, or "weighty Friends," as they were referred to, but that's ancient history.

The dynamic silence that characterizes the meeting for worship is a central and nearly sacred part of the event. Instead of a sermon, the silence is broken when anyone in attendance rises up to share whatever may be on his or her mind. We call this "vocal ministry," and we listen to it with caring and respect. The message may have glowingly spiritual dimensions that can set the theme for related ministry. There is a risk involved, of course, because there are rare occasions when the ministry may turn out to be contentious or vapid. We try to handle that with love and tenderness. The silent communion is what counts in the long run. Western culture has popularized the "moment of silence" for memorial events of tragedy, but we often have that moment before a meal. It's good to remember that if dining with Quakers—you won't need to break the ice with a joke if there's an "awkward" period of silence before eating.

So, what do Quakers believe, or what principles have usually been cobbled into our way of life? William Penn, the famous Quaker who founded our City of Brotherly Love, as well as my beloved University of Pennsylvania, said (as legend has it) that Quakers believe in the Fatherhood of God, the Brotherhood of Man, and the Neighborhood of Philadelphia. More seriously, however, I'll say that our *Faith and Practice* book answers the questions a lot better, but, briefly, I'll try to highlight some of the special features here. We don't have outward sacraments like confirmations and communion. This is *not* a rejection of many of those beautiful rites, rituals, and traditions—it is, rather, an assertion that we believe that the whole of life is sacramental. Oh, yes, we do make a big deal out of Christmas, but with a much greater focus on the prayer for peace on earth instead of elegant Nativity scenes. Other thoughts that I'll leave for later on in this book deal with Quaker attitudes and actions concerning social concerns related to the poor and dispossessed among us, a lifestyle of simplicity such that we avoid ostentatious living and an excessive compulsion to acquire material things, and a vigorous dedication to peace by actively working to take away the causes of war.

Although my tenure as clerk of Providence monthly meeting was a time of spiritual growth, it hardly qualifies me as a theologian or philosopher. Hence, these essays are not about that. They are intended to be nothing more or less than the peculiar reflections of a physical chemist who cherishes his religious identity as a Quaker—a Friend who would have his beliefs and values come from that powerful center we call the meeting for worship and who has a conviction that there is "that of God" in everyone. This belief that there is "that of God" in all people is alternately called the "essence of the divine," the "inner light," the "Christ within," or a similar variation. This is a kind of spiritual reality that cannot be described in any physical sense. In these writings, I will attempt to formulate a reconciliation between science and decidedly nontraditional Christian theology and to show how my identity as a Quaker is born in that union. And then I will attempt to illustrate how this identity rests totally on my philosophical cornerstone, which is an unrestricted respect for the sacredness and miraculous nature of *all* conscious beings.

The central parts of my widely divergent theses focus on the influence of Quaker principles on charting a course through the complexities of life. As is to be expected in a spiritual search phenomenon such as this, there will be few conclusions. Instead, I will be trying to ask some questions that need to be asked. *Large Circles and Bold Lines* has everything to do with the circles we draw to mark the boundaries between inclusions and exclusions in our lives. And the other question deals with our choices of where we draw the lines in an effort to discriminate among ideas, beliefs, and events. How can we know and apply the spiritual criteria that help us separate the significant from the trivial and determine what is right and true as opposed to what is fantasy and illusion?

Search for the Interface between Spiritual and Physical Reality

R*eality* is a common word that rolls easily off the tongue. It's a patchwork of symbols made into three syllables we can utter and feel confident that we know exactly what *reality* means. But, like most symbols, it can signify anything or nothing until we assign meaning to it. In the macro world around us there is no ambiguity. Reality is what we perceive through our senses. My car is a reality (though cheap and dented). Even at midnight we know the coming sunrise is a reality. Birth, growth, and death are realities. And so on . . . . But in the frontiers of particle physics and cosmology, we have only our feeble speculation on levels of reality that are beyond human experience. Time and space seem periodically to stretch and contract. Cause and effect appear to be mysterious and contradictory. The distinction between matter and energy blurs into a sameness—a single coin with two sides.

Physical Reality

My inability to relate to an awesome, omnipotent creator we call God derives in large part from my scientific orientation. It has little to do with scientific methodology, tangible proofs, demonstrable cause and effect, and the like. Rather, it's about my very limited ability to understand, visualize, or begin to cope with mind-boggling measurements and descriptions of natural phenomena in terms of time, space, mass, and energy—trying to deal with the distinctions between physical reality and the interactions among the entities that compose our palpable universe. The famous Danish physicist Neils Bohr could provide no definition of "reality." The brilliant Richard Feynman suggested that questions about the behavior of particles in the subatomic realm are better not asked.

"Don't ask how it (Quantum mechanics) can be like that. Nobody knows how it can be like that."

Men like Bohr and Feynman, who I regard as truly wise, understand the beauty of mystery and the creative power of ignorance in addressing the mysteries. Niels Bohr is commonly regarded as one of the most significant developers of modern atomic theory. He was a professor of physics at the University of Copenhagen, and his contributions were honored by the creation of the Niels Bohr Institute for Theoretical Physics.

Richard Feynman, acknowledged as a great professor of physics at Cal Tech, could also play bongo drums and perform safe cracking stunts with the best of them. An amazing guy!

A turning point for me started back in the late 1960s when I took a course in high energy particle physics at the Fermilab in Chicago. A new world started to open before my eyes, and I was enfolded within the arms of excitement and discovery. I started to learn about the application of units of measurement for things and events that ranged from unimaginably small or short to the large and distant that for most of us lie beyond the powers of imagination—and well beyond the powers of our most advanced microscopes, telescopes, and computer imaging capability.

Even cute analogies, such as the one that tries to give us some sense of how small an atom is, boggle the mind. For example, if we could take all the carbon atoms in a small half ounce lump of coal and blow them up so that each atom was the size of a marshmallow, we would have enough marshmallows to cover the whole continent of Australia to a depth of over six hundred miles!Think about the millions upon millions of star systems and galaxies that stretch across a universe in which it is hopeless to visualize distances. I like the way Hollywood's own Woody Allen concludes that, *"The universe is merely a fleeting idea in God's mind—a pretty uncomfortable thought, particularly if you've just made a down payment on a house."*

On a universal scale, the distance between Earth and the Sun is remarkably short. Yet it takes the light from the

Sun more than eight minutes to reach us. That light is traveling 186,000 miles per second! It's a distance of more than ninety million miles. And we thought a few hundred miles to visit relatives was a big trip. But then our distance from the Sun, compared to distances between galaxies, is practically nothing! Intergalactic distances can be measured with impressive accuracy, but that doesn't give us more than a mathematical notation which amounts to a big, fat intellectual abstraction. There is simply nothing, nor is it likely that there will ever be anything in our experience, that can permit us to grasp the concept of the distance that light travels over a period of millions of years.

I find myself overwhelmed by the mechanical energy of Niagara Falls, and I am left breathless by the massiveness of Mount Kanchenjunga in the Himalayas, but how puny they are in comparison to the mass of a planet and the size of a star. And I wonder why it is that way and how can it be like that? The brilliant and eccentric Professor Feynman came up with a lovely mixed metaphor that responds to my questions. He was talking about quantum theory, but I think it applies here,

"Do not keep saying to yourself . . . . 'But how can it be like that?' because you will get down the drain, into a blind alley from which nobody has escaped. Nobody knows how it can be like that."

Moving from the mind-bending realm of universal sizes and distances, I'm equally astounded by intra-atomic measurements at the other end of the scale. Unusual metric units had to be applied because a millionth of a second is much too long a time to describe events related to the big bang birth of our universe in which the "soup" of matter and antimatter particles were so small that using millimeter units would be as inappropriate as measuring a virus in miles. Quantum theory, which is a way of describing the physics of basic natural phenomena, must use units of measurements that go far beyond what we could ever hope to visualize. Albert Einstein, the world's iconic genius, said,

"This Quantum theory reminds me a little of a system of delusions of an exceedingly intelligent paranoic, concocted of incoherent elements of thought."

Even though my head is spinning, the fires of curiosity will burn brightly and enrich my life, but I need to look for other kinds of miracles if it's possible to find God. Moving into the realm of possibilities and probability, I can escape from the prison of classical structures and deterministic laws. With that step, I can function more in tune with my inner stirrings and primal instincts, which the ultimate miracle of human consciousness permits. There is something called an anthropic principle that intrigues modern scientists. There are actually several variations of this principle, but the one that most appeals to me is the one that suggests that, from the creation of the universe in the big bang, the laws of nature have evolved so that life can exist. And from the simplest of life-forms, conscious beings like you and me could arise to be the observers of it all. Astounding that out of an unimaginably cataclysmic eruption of a singular point of seething, turbulent nothingness, our universe could take shape! And then, with the passing of eons, it could produce a perfect balance among the variable forces that govern the interactions between units of matter and energy so that replicating life-forms were able to evolve from the cosmic dust.

With some audacity and with no pretense of a systematic study or argument here, I want to talk more about the universe—as best I can without the severe restrictions of esoteric language and mathematics. I am overwhelmed by its immensity and fascinated by speculations about its birth and possible extinction eventually. Or will the universe continue to expand forever? And the other extreme in so far as sizes go is the atom and the little bitty parts of atoms that dazzle us with an array of interactions defying us to grind out a grand theory of everything. We have developed a wary eye on our reductionist tendency that would take us into the absurd—absurd because if we tried to pare the atom down to its simplest units (i.e., reductionism) and the universe to nothingness, we still would have to contend with the enigmatic statement of the American John Wheeler, a prominent Princeton University physicist who coined the term black hole, who said,

"No point is more central than this, that empty space is not empty. It is the seat of the most violent physics." Far from being empty, current cosmological theory suggests that the universe is filled with a vast amount of mysterious dark matter.

Today, a preponderance of evidence leads most scientists to believe that all space, time, and matter (i.e., the universe) came into existence in a "big bang"—an indescribable explosion of a point of infinite energy about fifteen billion years ago and still expanding and congealing into matter. And some still believe it all will end in a "big crunch." This is total annihilation. Nothing is left. No places, no moments, no things. There is a final *singularity* as all of existence succumbs to the awesome destructive power of gravity, and then, no more. I've seen it written somewhere that gravity, the midwife of the cosmos, may also be its undertaker.

Even more mind-boggling than "bangs" and "crunches" is the ultimate contrast between intra-atomic dimensions and the size of the universe. Distances are measured in light years and multiples of light years in astronomical units called "parsecs." On the atomic level we measure things in fractions of attometres—an attometre being a quintillionth of a metre, written as a decimal point followed by seventeen zeros before the number one.

There is indeed something almost morbid and tragic about our tendency to brood over the end of things. But then I recall the curiously reassuring comment by the American Nobel laureate Steven Weinberg, who said, *"The effort to understand the universe is one of the very few things that lifts human life a little above the level of a farce, and gives it some of the grace of tragedy."*

Weinberg is also quite famous as a Harvard professor of theoretical physics, and, in a philosophical sense, he is a staunch humanist.

It may be that the poetical inclinations of scientists soften the blows to their *a priories* and the kicks to their *a posteriories.* In any case, we don't look for common sense explanations of cosmic mystery. It may be worth remembering that Einstein said (tongue-in-cheek notwithstanding), *"Common sense is a layer of prejudice you acquire by the age of sixteen."*

The preservation of our species and this planet we call home may depend critically on how successful we are in bringing a childlike curiosity about our universe and an aesthetic sensitivity to the search for some insights into the meaning of physical reality.Now, any reference to modern physics requires use of the term *quantum theory.* That's the starting point. These days we have the added the joys of string theory, multiple universes, and supersymmetry, but that can wait .... So, in a feeble effort to reduce professorial hand-waving and guru-like posturing, let me say a few words about what quantum theory is and what it tries to do. Quantum theory is an abstract attempt to say something about nature as it is inextricably tied to and affected by us as observers. It is primarily about physical reality on the subatomic level. Quantum theory deals with forces between subatomic particles and related energy changes. Pragmatically, quantum theory has been enormously successful in the advancement of modern technology. The novel features of quantum theory such as: the particle nature of precise amounts of energy (which is what a quantum is); instantaneous changes between quantum particles by ethereal carriers, or *mediators*; the dual nature of waves and particles (complementarity); and particle creation are all handled in terms of statistical probabilities. Quantum mechanics uses mathematical formalisms to apply laws that supposedly govern the behavior of matter and energy. On the atomic level, and within the constraints of quantifiable uncertainties, these laws seem to work where the laws of classical Newtonian physics fail.

Denmark's Niels Bohr, one of the great physicists of the twentieth century, interpreted physical reality as something having meaning only if it could be observed. It may be a solipsistic notion, but John Wheeler supported his interpretation of quantum theory with the words, *"Observers may be necessary to bring the universe into being."*

Bohr actually said, *"The existence of the world out there is not something that enjoys an independence of its own, but is inextricably tied up with our perception of it."* And if we ask what the characteristics of an observer are, the Austro-Hungarian Nobel laureate Eugene Wigner answers by saying that an observer must have

". . . . the self-reflective property of human consciousness." Wigner adds, *"It is not possible to formulate the laws of quantum mechanics in a fully consistent way without reference to consciousness . . . . Solipsism is consistent with quantum mechanics because the results of an observation modify the probabilities of later observations; this is where consciousness enters."*

Earlier in the twentieth century the French Count Louis de Broglie, a great French physics professor at the famous Sorbonne, wrote, *"In every epoch in the history of science, aesthetic feeling has been a guide—that has directed scientists in their research."*

Werner Heisenberg, a student of Bohr, became the reluctant leader of the Nazi atomic bomb project during the Second World War. It was an intensely wrenching drama in which Heisenberg had to compromise his humanitarian instincts, as well as his friendship with his mentor, by choosing to remain loyal to his fatherland. Many of Heisenberg's contemporaries believed his inner moral conflicts finally led him to purposefully fail to complete his work.

On a much happier note during better times, Heisenberg confirmed de Broglie's thought in his own words by saying, "

. . . . beauty in exact science, no less that the arts . . . . is the most important source of illumination and clarity."

More recently, Richard Feynman declared that

". . . . in science you can recognize truth by its beauty, simplicity, and symmetry."

According to the Canadian authors Robert Augros and George Stanciu, philosophy and "new biology" professors at St. Anselm College, there are three basic elements of beauty: simplicity, harmony, and brilliance. The brilliance of both physical theory and the various fine arts link clearly to the standards of symmetry and simplicity. Britain's Paul Davies adds,

"In constructing their theories, physicists are frequently guided by arcane concepts of elegance in the belief that the universe is intrinsically beautiful."

Davies was a physics professor and author of many popular science books while at Cambridge University. One of his outstanding books, called *God and the New Physics*, which is on my shelf at home, is a thought-provoking excursion into the world of metaphysics. I find a number of parallels between the beliefs of Davies and myself that still exist although I read his book years ago.

Mathematics is properly called the language of science. Even in its most abstract and esoteric forms we can be overwhelmed by its inherent simplicity and harmony. There are, however, additional dimensions to its beauty, and we find these, for example, in the mysteries of imaginary numbers, the paradoxes of correct solutions to equations that yield impossible answers, and the mind-boggling concept of infinity.

Max Planck, the German Nobelist and Berlin University professor who gave birth to the quantum theory about a century ago, was remarkably on target many years ago when he wrote, *"Science cannot solve the ultimate mystery of Nature. And it is because in the last analysis, we ourselves are part of the mystery we are trying to solve."*

A related argument is described by the Australian astrophysicist Brandon Carter as the anthropic principle. Some scientists regard this principle with a jaundiced eye and charitably call it metaphysics, at best. However, I am intrigued, and I find some power in it as it states, *"The universe must be such to admit conscious beings in it at some stage. This amounts to saying that, far from being unlikely, the universe had no choice about appearing with the degree of order required for life to appear. And this universe we perceive is only one of a huge collection of universes. Among this collection of universes we have every possible arrangement of matter and energy of which only a minute fraction have the right conditions for the emergence of human consciousness."*

The "reality" of black holes, big bangs, and the unification of forces morph inexorable into philosophical reality . . . . and this is where I am. I don't know who thought it or said it first, but in the philosophical realm of beliefs and values it has been said that we create our own realities. I subscribe to this notion.

I am skeptical about the merit of choosing to believe in absolutes. Among the few absolutes I subscribe to, and one that I will write about here, is the nature of my belief in the existence of a creative intelligence, which I see as the eternal architect of all things and all life. I call this nebulous entity "God." I cannot begin to divine the purpose or plan of this God, and I will not try. Professing belief in God will earn me no merit badge or public approval because, by the conventional standards of the world's major religions, my belief is unequivocally heretical. Saying, "I believe God exists," may come off like a resounding affirmation of faith, but I admit to myself that taken out of a larger context, it is quite meaningless.

Let me reiterate here, for the sake of clarity and emphasis, the essence of what I've said about an anthropic principle as it provides a possible bridge between the worlds of science and religion. I believe the reality of God relates directly to the probability that all the physical conditions essential to the rise and spread of life-forms had to be "just right" within narrow limits. Such an incredible phenomenon allows for a "leap of faith" in which I believe that our lives could not have resulted from a highly improbable cosmic accident. Life is such a mind-boggling negation of chaos—a dramatic contradiction of some basic laws of classical physics. Cosmological empirical data increasingly support the theory that the expansion of our universe is a story of evolution from the stark simplicity of "nothingness" before time and place existed to the incredible complexity we see today. I have no special attachment to monotheism. Regarding the trinitarian variation, I can just say, "Been there, done that," but no longer find it particularly meaningful. Nor do I have any special regard for the volumes of "sacred writ" venerated by people for millennia. To me, revered icons like the Bible or the Koran are books of poetry, allegorical tales, didactic parables, flawed accounts of gory historical events, and a thick file of anachronistic guides for living a moral life. All of which I see as amounting to considerably less than "The Word of God."

If any notion can come close to describing my concept of the nature of God, it is a kind of pantheism in which I believe that the essence of God is in the whole of creation. However, that generalization is so nebulous. It is abstract and inconsequential. It describes a vision of a deity that I cannot relate to in a way that makes God an active and meaningful presence in my life.It is in the miracle of conscious beings that I find the tangible expression of God. It is only in my fellow human beings that I can experience the nature of God. It is in all people, both good and bad—encompassing the whole spectrum of humanity from beloved saints to despicably depraved tyrants. What is most powerful and meaningful to me is finding God in my family, friends, and acquaintances. In a larger, but less personal sense, I believe that there is "that of God" in all conscious beings.

Reflections on the Nature of God

As I grow older, I'm increasingly startled by what I believe is my diminishing capacity for wisdom and certainty—a kind of epiphany of inverse proportionality between stupidity and ignorance. It is, of course, possible to be both stupid and ignorant, but I prefer to cling to my perception of there more likely being 180 degrees of separation between the two. In any case, I'd rather not suppress my innate optimism. The wiser I'm supposed to become with age and experience, the less sure I am about how my life might better fit into the "larger scheme of things." I need to rethink and revise my positions constantly in order to get some stability in a value system that for me is always in a state of readjustment. I'm looking for enough light to deal with the shadowy fear that my life may become insignificant and trivial.

These musings are *vis-à-vis* questions dealing with the nature of being, the nature of God, physical and spiritual "reality," and the meaning and purpose of life. Much of what has been governing my thinking for years, and what I'm partly trying to set forth here in words, is a principle of uncertainty—not what Werner Heisenberg promulgated as a description of subatomic particle interaction, but a philosophical application he never intended. This is, admittedly, a stretch. But I find it useful to work from a standpoint of uncertainty as my own personal defense against getting sucked into a world of philosophical absolutes limited by logical positivism (i.e., nonmystical, empirical knowledge) and reductionist attitudes which demand that all things must be explained in terms of cause and effect. I prefer not to look for limits and boundaries to what is possible. Although I may harbor serious doubts and be skeptical about the "truth" and merit of human claims and achievements, I allow for the possible happening of almost anything the mind of man can imagine. While I remain highly skeptical about the invention of "time machines," human levitation by willpower, or a geographical place in space-time called "heaven," to mention a few phenomena that people have dreamed of, I do remember when I scoffed at the notions of Buck Rogers's spaceship and Dick Tracy's wrist radio. Even more astounding is the realization that we have technological and medical advances that were probably beyond the scope of most people's imagination fifty years ago.

Some of the most profound and important questions in life, as I see it, are the ones for which I have no answers. And I say that without any inclination toward self-effacement or rhetorical trickery. When I was a child, I did have lots of answers. All of them were very pat, logical, and meriting approval from the morally and religiously correct sages who had taught me a kind of catechism in which the true answer was supplied for every heavy question—literal believers who insist that since heaven exists, it must be *somewhere*.

The passing of a child's view of the world is tinged with a bit of sadness, however. It's a time when we tend to be so spontaneous, so easily filled with astonishment, wonder, and exuberance as we learn about the beauty and mystery of nature. But as we grow, we become aware of the complexities of life and begin to have doubts about Santa Claus and the comforting wisdom of old homilies that we had recited in tones reserved for "holy scripture." We begin to doubt and challenge. Perhaps we even dare to scoff and sneer at notions and beliefs that people hold as "eternal verities." The small sadness is inescapable because as we grow and learn, we experience a disconcerting change in life. A sense of awe and the thrill of discovery are being displaced by an evolving spirit of cynicism and suspicion directed toward parental and biblical authority. The simple beliefs of a child are deeply ingrained within the core of our beings, and this makes it difficult, to the point of being traumatic, if we react negatively to the beliefs and values we were taught. Any dramatic rejections will likely lead to some elements of guilt and the fear that we may be cutting ourselves adrift from a solid attachment to the rituals and traditions of family and friends. But change will happen as long as there is the courage to seek truth and question authority. Change was the hallmark of my own effort to formulate a uniquely personal value system and theological subscription. Things were always in a state of flux, with never any conviction that a declaration of "Here I stand!" was ready to be nailed to some public wall. What did come was a willingness to deal with personal contradictions, accusations of classical heresy, and philosophical absurdities, and even an eagerness to take irrational walks out on a slippery slope.

Philosophically, my lifelong quest for enlightenment continues to be a liberation from the strictures of religious, political, and behavioral correctness. My life embodies the exuberance of feeling free of the need to maintain postures of dignity and decorum, to challenge and even selectively disregard items of conventional morality (also called family values), and to no longer live with the inhibitions that deny the chances to act like a fool or a clown. It includes the joy of humor without special regard for the rules laid down by the thin-skinned types who insist on being socially "correct" and who are, perhaps, too easily offended. The ancient concepts of "heresy" and "blasphemy" are still used as bludgeons to mangle the more joyful instincts we need to enrich our lives.

God and Human Consciousness

The existence of human consciousness is to me the greatest miracle that could ever be. There may be other forms of conscious beings "out there," in some other corner of our galaxy or beyond, but it seems so irrelevant. The idea piques my curiosity, and I wonder about life on another planet as a matter of idle speculation. Even if it turns out to be true, I can't see that it adds or subtracts from the miracle that we are. For without conscious beings to perceive our universe and marvel at its magnificence and be affected by it, the whole business of universal creation is reduced to a meaningless cosmic farce. Without conscious beings, there is nothing. Who could validate the existence of mountains and call them mighty? Who could be overwhelmed by the vastness of the sea or the heat of the Sun? Who could be astonished by the sight of the stars in the sky if there is, indeed, no "who" to be the observer of it all?It is so amazing to realize how the apparent suspension of natural law has allowed for the development of extraordinarily complex beings out of a chaos of particle interactions. Specifically, the laws of thermodynamics must be considered here (without being too technical). The first law is about energy conservation, and it says, in effect, that we can't get something for nothing. No magical machines are out there that can give us more energy than we put in. The second law is more grim; it states that the physical chaos (or, randomness, disorder) of our material world is destined to increase. And the third law is positively depressing by declaring that it is not possible to do anything about it. The three laws, paraphrased as simple-mindedly as possible, can be listed in order as: (1) you can't win, (2) you can't break even, and (3) you can't even get out of the game. So, in effect, it is the second law of thermodynamics that says that we cannot *be*. But we *are*, and without us there is nothing, no stars, no mountains, no mystery, no beauty—nothing. After all, what does "beauty" matter if there is no conscious being to observe it, be a part of it, and say *wow!*

This is why I believe that God has made us. And so I ask, "What is the nature of this God? Are we, indeed, made in the image of God such that disparate traits like a sense of humor or vindictiveness are a part of this divine being? Where can I find this God? Is he/she a human-like being living in a kind of heaven above the clouds? Is he embodied in the historical Jesus hanging on a cross? Is he/she a spirit . . . . a universal, intangible spirit we call 'Love'? Or an infinite body of absolute intelligence that created everything?" I don't pretend to know, of course. All I can do is offer my respect for anyone's right to believe whatever makes any sense to them. For myself, all I can do is admit that I don't have the foggiest notion of whether or not God is supposed to be some kind of describable "being." This is why I can only find the indescribable essence of the "Divine" in the miracle of human consciousness.

What, then, does God want of me? Why did God create conscious beings at all? I don't know, but I suspect that God made us because it is through our senses and emotions that God can perceive the magnitude and beauty of what has been created. So, the very essence of God must reside within us, otherwise it is all so empty and meaningless. Who could care about the most wondrous creations if there is no "who" to care?

For the beliefs that people have, I'm not inclined to ridicule and scoff. I just know that I cannot relate in a personal way to the omnipotent creator and ruler of the universe. In my own theological development, subject as it is to ongoing modification, I simply am more comfortable with a pantheism. I don't know if "comfortable" is the best word, but I am unable to subscribe to and believe in any of the classically monotheistic religions.

Here then, is where my Quaker identity is rooted. Although there is no set of beliefs or creedal statement in Quakerism that one is obliged to accept, there is one widely held belief that comes close. It is the belief that there is something of God in everyone. Regardless of age, gender, level of saintliness or depravity, there is a sacred aspect to every human. I've taken this seventeenth century revelation out of context, but "that of God in everyone" is at the core of my attitude toward life—human life in particular. This is, emphatically, a philosophical or theological construct. The concept of "that of God in everyone" is inherently paradoxical and mystical. There is no adequate explanation for, or description of, this "essence." Perhaps the concept of a "soul" is somewhat analogous. The paradox comes out because with a few portentous words we can say it all, while in an analytical context we are saying nothing at all. The meaning to the individual can be powerful despite the fact that we know that there is no tangible "God-stuff" or "soul tissue" within us.

The implications of my subscribing to the concept of "that of God in everyone" are quite significant to me.

It necessarily affects my attitude and behavior toward people. Part of this is probably related to my temperament, which leads me toward interactions in which I can revel in an environment of camaraderie, *joie de vivre*, humorous banter, and so on. It defines the concept of respect. Either by temperament or a gentle sense of caring, I am compelled to be optimistic—to look for what is good in a person, to give them the benefit of any doubt regarding their motives, and to accept them at face value without looking for sinister undertones. I want to be publicly nonjudgmental and see eccentric people as being "different" rather than "weird" or "off the wall" and being targets for ridicule and snide remarks. I always hope that my efforts toward civilized behavior might even mature into genuine feelings of warmth and affection. I have a long way to go *vis-à-vis* my own defects in character, but I'm reasonably content with who I am, to the point that I am able to abide my many imperfections without being consumed by a paralyzing feeling of guilt. I've pretty much concluded that I have neither the will nor the saintliness to hunger and thirst after righteousness. It's almost a perverse realization of Billy Joel's choice when he sings that he'd rather party with the sinners than hang out with the saints. It is within each individual in the whole community of conscious beings that I find the God with whom I can relate in a way in which I cannot relate to a cosmic, omnipotent supreme being somewhere "out there." It is a cornerstone in my pantheistic structure to believe that the essence of God within us engenders an attitude of profound respect for human dignity. This enables me to give respect as a gift without strings attached—no expectation of reciprocation or requirement that my respect must be earned. It is my conscious choice to do it this way because it is simply the way I have to live.

The Evolution of an Identity

My decision to identify myself with Quakerism was one of the most significant moves in my life. It was a major step in the choosing of my own destiny that took place over sixty years ago—a more than half-century of time that continues to confirm the "rightness" of what I did. In turning away from a birthright heritage that would have allowed me to rejoice in and celebrate the customs, rituals, and traditions of my family, I chose to let a new identity evolve—one that is uniquely mine. It's a religious identity that "speaks to my condition" and mirrors my attitudes and beliefs. When I attended my first meeting for worship, I was overwhelmed and felt engulfed by human warmth that was so real and without expectations. I was deeply moved by the simplicity of the experience. There were none of the traditional characteristics of a typical house of worship—no altar, banners, leader, prayer books, stained glass, or statues and symbols. Instead, there was just an expectant silence in place of the usual liturgical order of religious services in which we parrot prescribed prayers, sing hymns, and participate in responsive readings devoted to reaffirming the glory and power of God. It was for me an epiphany. I knew then and there that I had found what I was looking for. In Quakerism I found a way of worship and a whole new way of life in which I seemed to fit. It was probably similar in a way to the evangelical born-again phenomenon from which a new identity begins to evolve.Quakerism is much more than can be expressed in any brief quasi-theological statement. The Quaker sect is indeed a religious organization that heralds attitudes and a lifestyle that give substance to a belief in the sacredness of life. There are cherished principles of simplicity, peacemaking, and social concerns related to equal justice and opportunity for all people. Quakerism eschews the outward trappings of "sacraments" like baptism, confirmation, and an ordained clergy—preferring to see the whole of life as sacramental. It's this and more without the baggage of ultrarighteousness and evangelical zealotry. We do not aspire to be a saintly cult of "do-gooders" or a select breed of high-minded intellectuals. In Quakerism, we try to live a kind of life that has its meeting for worship as the central "powerhouse" of all its genuine caring, warmth, and affection. For me, Quakerism has become that singular religious component of my identity.

The importance of identity can hardly be overstated. Furthermore, I believe that in this day and age, religion is much more a matter of identity than it is about theological belief. The secure feeling that we each have a unique identity is routinely assumed to be a given. The importance, however, is often underrated. We not only need to have a sense of identity, but many of us feel a need to proclaim a delineation of our "root" connections, such as race, religion, nationality, and ethnicity. We announce who we are by the organizations we belong to, the neighborhood in which we live, and the nature of our job or profession. We wear our identity like badges in the way we talk, dress, and by what we favor in things like music, food, and leisure activity. Our identity emerges by virtue of the kinds of people with whom we associate—people who more than likely share our interests and values. It seems to be part of our human nature to fulfill this need to know who we are and what we stand for.

Some of us find fascination in the discovery and defining of our ancestral roots. Adopted individuals can become obsessed with finding out their biological origins. I believe that the quest for an identity is a primal urge, even more vital to us than a need to impress others with things like our achievements, victories, brilliance, and whatever other real or imagined bragging rights we might claim. I think, too, that the assumption of an identity is driven in large part by a need to reassure ourselves that we do in fact exist, that others care about us, and that we count for something.I suspect that one of the most demoralizing and frustrating experiences a person can have is when he is in the company of others who act as though he's invisible. It must be a feeling of excruciating loneliness, even within a crowd of people, when no one seems to hear this person or care at all about what he may have to say. This is the kind of scenario in which one starts to become overwhelmed by doubts about his existence as a significant being. It's a dreadful feeling of having one's dignity stripped away until he's reduced to a nonentity, not worthy of recognition or respect. That's an extreme scenario, yes, but one intended to restate emphatically the importance of a sense of identity.

There are aspects of our identity that, in a Shakespearean sense, are thrust upon us by virtue of our birth—nationality, race, ethnicity, socioeconomic status, and so on. Other components of our identity are chosen in response to our dreams, interests, and aspirations—becoming a jock, a musician, an artist, a leader of some sort, or serendipitously discovering something in life that had never been anticipated.

Quakerism is for me the central religious component of my identity. In lieu of a creed, it means a joyful attachment to customs and traditions, along with simple and enduring rituals that were in place centuries before my arrival on the scene. Being a Quaker is for me a bold announcement of the kind of person I want my identity to reflect in terms of my stewardship of the few but cherished traditions that characterize the popular conception of Quakerism. The Quaker attitude, however, would never wish to trivialize the beauty and sacredness of mainstream religious rituals and traditions.

A Perception of Miracle

The discovery of my perception of "miracle" was partly serendipitous and partly a consequence of my trying to deal with that dreadful question of why a supposedly loving God allows bad things to happen to good people. We ask how there can be any purpose in God's choosing anyone to be afflicted by some undeserved tragedy (if that is God's "plan"). Many people find no satisfactory answer in organized religion. Even the inspirational stories of physically and mentally disabled people who found that God had some wonderful purpose don't assuage the pain. Maybe the dumbest thing we can do is ask *why*. There may be some noble and glorious reason for it all, but we don't know what it is. We hope, somehow, in ways and for reasons beyond the power of our imagination, that the grace of God is operative in human grief and suffering.

Like countless others, I've had to deal with the seemingly awful contradiction of belief in a loving God who permits suffering and tragedy. My daughter, Lise, had been born with cerebral palsy, and, in spite of her never ending battle with pain, frustration, and spastic quadriplegia, she absolutely radiated a joyful enthusiasm for life. Finally, the time came when her body could no longer cope with a dreadfully heavy regimen of drugs and string of hospital surgeries, and we lost our precious daughter. There were times before Lise's freedom from suffering when she looked into my eyes, the eyes of her dad, who she believed could answer any question, and she asked, "Why me?" I had no answer, of course. I think I said something to the effect that there are some questions that are better left unasked because the simplistic answers we hear from well-meaning people don't work for us. Many genuinely kind and pious people believe that God is purposeful in all things that happen, but I find that too much of a stretch. I'll write more about this later on in the essay titled "Another Kind of Circle."

Centuries of religion have given us great music, art, and architecture. The grand houses of worship have enabled the poor and dispossessed to taste vicariously the grandeur and glory of organized religion. The millions who live in hovels and scratch for food can bask in the reflected power of ecclesiastical trappings—the revered priesthood, the mighty cathedrals, and all the ritual pageantry that contribute to their identity. And with it all, there's the hope for miracles, the hopes and prayers addressed to saints and angels who might intercede with God so they can be taken magically to a better life —or a better hereafter. The obvious virtues of organized religion help to ameliorate the negative sting when religions are used to divide people into warring camps, to fuel the venomous agenda of fanatical zealots, and to relieve people of the need to think and evaluate for themselves. And there's so much empty gesture, hocus-pocus, and hand-waving hypocrisy to blur our perceptions of where meaningful religion ends and religiosity begins.

Religiosity, however, is for many people much more than a vapid "going through the motions" of appearing pious and reverential. Observance of customs and traditions provides many with a strong link to their identity. The performance of historical rituals can be a source of deep comfort as a convincing validation of one's religious roots. Even people who reject the precepts of their church, temple, mosque, zendo, or whatever, feel a sense of loyalty and continuity in maintaining family traditions. Totally inactive members of a particular religion or sect may opt for events like baptism, bar mitzvah, confirmation, and marriage because of a sense of fidelity to their roots.

It may come out of a sense of guilt even if there is no viable attachment to a particular faith. It may be due to a vision of God that was ingrained at childhood so that a lurking, unspoken fear remains that the Old Man is still up there in heaven and writing down transgressions in "the book." A particular tradition, such as marriage, for example, might emerge as a wonderful (and often expensive) reason for a celebration, replete with all the appropriate food, music, and revelry. Religious traditions may involve denial, fasting, and abstinence, but the clear expression of one's identity has a value that cannot be invented or measured even though it comes out in the form of religiosity.

Instead of agonizing over the distinction between piety and religiosity, we can more usefully focus on the miracles that fill our lives with joy. This is not a thing we can analyze and explain, because its nature lies in the basic mystery of brain-mind-soul interaction. We grasp some meaning, intuitively, but we don't really understand. Let me address this concept of miracle by looking at a single phenomenon—a precious fragment of our reality—which is a smile. It's the smile that enabled my daughter to light up the world all the years of her life, and it's the smile that still lights up my world when I look at her picture. It is one miracle among so many, and it's the kind of miracle that dwarfs the popular miracles of the saints and the self-proclaimed miracle workers who, by the laying on of hands, or the incantation of their mumbo jumbo, cause the lame to walk, the blind to see, and even the dead to rise again. Miracles like visitations from God in a burning bush, the parting of the Red Sea, or battlefield victories by small bands of "believers" over the mighty hordes of godless infidels seem like cheap carnival tricks compared to the miracle of human consciousness.

A Perspective on Circles

There must be dozens of ways in which we use the word *circle* in figures of speech like a *circle* of friends or the family *circle*. We have a geometrical icon which has no beginning or end and with a distinct radius that describes the border between what is within and what is outside. The radius is everything. There is the tight radius to encompass the select few. It defines the term *exclusivity* by functioning as a boundary between *us* and *them*. It reassures us of an intrinsic value among our peers and it affirms the special merit of our identity.

If the tendency to draw small, exclusive circles was simply a matter of brotherhood or camaraderie or the fulfillment of a primitive sense of belonging, we'd be comfortable saying that it was natural and quite consistent with the better parts of our human nature. But when it becomes a line that marks a boundary between the "true believers" and the "infidels," the aristocracy and the peasants, the cultured and the boorish, the "haves" and "have-nots," and so on, it begins to encompass some of the elements of societal despair and degeneration.

Or worse, such as when our exclusive circles are drawn in a time of war to indicate which side God is on. With the power of prayer, the armor of righteousness, and a cultivated arrogance, we can justify massive destruction and the killing, maiming, and vilification of those barbarians outside the circle. Before getting into my predictable antiwar polemic, let me reach out for a broader perspective. Real-life scenes that we paint with bold brushstrokes of black and white simplify things, but in our zealous quest for absolutes we easily overlook, or even deny, that life has many shades of gray and a whole spectrum of colors. The acknowledgment of colors and shades of gray requires a willingness to walk out onto the *slippery slope* and maintain balance in the face of wrath and ridicule. The "silent majority" will probably not remain so silent. In a world populated by the "politically correct" and all manner of religious zealots who know exactly what the word of God is, condemnation will be amply provided.And so it is *vis-à-vis* the question of war. Traditionally, we tend to think of all wars as a conflict between good and evil or an expression of the darker side of human nature. This is a sweeping generalization that I challenge. We like to believe that we are always the "good guys" with a just cause—to liberate the oppressed, remove tyrants, restore freedom, and, of course, make the world safe for democracy. More recent additions to this litany of salvation include the elimination of terrorism and the confiscation of weapons of mass destruction. I see merit in these aspirations, but I cannot accept war as a means toward that end. To talk of war as a last resort and proceed to justify sanctimoniously the use of "pre-emptive strikes," smacks of monumental hypocrisy. The portrayal of Saddam Hussein as a neo-Hitler is, to me, a distortion of reality and a feeble justification for usurping the prerogatives of the United Nations. Hitler was a megalomaniacal monster who had to be stopped before he fulfilled his goal of conquering the world and eliminating more millions of non-Aryans. He might have been stopped before his war machine was rebuilt and before the Western nations pursued the failed effort to appease. But the clear vision of hindsight is little more than a frustrating intellectual exercise. A war did, in fact, engulf us, and it was one that had to be justified once the point of no return had passed in 1938. A *just* war? Okay, I'll walk out on the slippery slope and agree that the deeds and lies of madmen bent on unprecedented "ethnic cleansing" had to be stopped by the methods of war. I will admit that had I been old enough to participate in World War II, I probably would have, but hopefully in a way that would have allowed me to save life—perhaps as a medic.

And then we have circles within circles. Circles that, in becoming tighter and tighter, cause Muslims to fractionate into Arab and non-Arab cultures, Sunnis and Shiites; the Jews into Orthodox and more liberal congregations; and Christians into Catholic, Protestant, and a further splitting into waves of evangelical born-again fundamentalists and the ongoing growth of bizarre cults. And this is only the beginning of the proliferation of circles within circles unless and until we can draw the larger, more inclusive circle that permits a gracious conciliation between the fact of diversity and the need for unity. Call it brotherhood or fraternity, if you prefer.

Diversity is a fact of life. It's a glorious one at that—with a dazzling variety of cultural and ethnic differences to enrich our lives. Think for a moment how the diverse cultures of the Latinos, Blacks, Mediterranean peoples, Middle Easterners, Appalachian folks, Slavs, Asians, etc. have contributed to the food, music, and lifestyles in America. Diversity also projects a larger spectrum of human variety, where we can find our own identity. But it can also be the root of strife, suspicion, hatred, and a dreadful feeling of hopelessness in which we see no alternative to the destruction of the enemy who we perceive as a threat to whatever it is that we stand for and identify with. It's a "them or us" mentality or an acquiescence to the "eye for an eye, tooth for a tooth" tragedy until blind and toothless adversaries grope their way through bitterness and wreckage as they try to find the road to sanity. Eventually, when civilizations have been trashed, when enough blood has been shed, and when the hopes and dreams of people are pathetic remnants of what they were, then maybe we will be moved to reaffirm our oneness as brothers and sisters who, in harmonious communion, honor that of God in each of us.

It boggles the mind that we are still able to accept the self-serving fiction of a *just* war with every adversary, each of whom believes that God is on their side—each side in its own way steeping themselves in prayer and sanctimonious posturing while they proceed to strip the sacredness and dignity of our species by killing and maiming in the name of God. Preemptive strikes are justified. Brutalizing captives and piously mourning the destruction of innocents due to "collateral damage" becomes regrettably part of the *game plan.*

We can say that war is a product of the primitive instinct for self-preservation, but we have been saying that throughout all the millennia of human history. It's a stultifying anachronism! War is such a breathtaking contradiction of human intelligence. Wisdom and sanity are left to rot on a stinking pile of arrogance and zealotry while the hawks and bigots of the world pound the drums of patriotic fervor and prate about the evil enemy who would take away our freedom and destroy our democracy.

I believe the great "victory" over the Al Qaeda/Iraqi threat to our American freedom is a case in point. I feel strongly that it was a war that was both unnecessary and unwise. It is a war that is costing us billions of dollars, a continuing loss of "coalition" lives, a much larger loss of Iraqi lives, and the killing and maiming of innocent civilians. And there is also the further demolishing of an infrastructure already in ruins because of the tyrannical leadership of a megalomaniacal dictator, a decade of economic sanctions, and many decades of amoral corruption. Have we gained any advantage for the Iraqi people by replacing a dictatorship with a theocracy that rants about fomenting a resurgence of Taliban-like repression?

Thus far, our "liberation" of the Iraqi people has yielded widespread resentment toward the liberators. They want us to get out. There is a mix of ignorance, fear, and the humiliation of defeat festering like a cancer on their Arab-Islamic manhood.

We saw how a hypocritical, self-serving administration regenerated a spirit of *rah-rah* patriotism that brought back chilling reminders of the Joe McCarthy era. And so Congress gave Bush the go-ahead to smite the *evildoers* and destroy their stockpiled weapons of mass destruction. In the rush to war, the UN was emasculated. A few nations that opted to give the search team of the UN time to do their work were reviled and ridiculed. An embarrassing assortment of *yahoos* and *ding-a-lings,* rallying behind Bush, Rumsfeld, and Chaney, called for actions like the boycott of French wines and the renaming of our popular potato sticks as *Freedom fries.*In the resulting chaos of war, the have-nots fall too easily into the irrational behavior of looting, rioting, and killing. The grim result is that we have not removed the horrors of terrorism. The Al Qaeda live and hover as a daily threat to innocent people. Suicide bombers aspire to martyrdom driven by despair, hopelessness, and a yearning for glory and praise they will never see. They are extremely vulnerable young people, susceptible to the exhortations of fanatical clergy who assure them of their heavenly reward in paradise.

The terrorist organizations like Hamas and Islamic Jihad continue to wage the "holy war"—one of the great oxymorons of all time. There's the unlikely alliance of ultraorthodox Israeli settlers and Christian fundamentalists, both justifying the claim to Arab territory as a fulfillment of a promise God made to the Hebrew people. Lawlessness and corruption continue unabated, if not increased. The hatred of us, our way of life, our institutions, and our culture grow without signs of diminution. There appears to be so much that might have been accomplished in a positive and constructive way and at a small fraction of what it is costing us in dollars, frustration, human casualties, and the propagation of so much ill will.

One side says *Allahu akbar*—"God is Great"—and God willing, we will drive out the infidels. The other side kneels before an image of Christ hanging on a cross and believes with holy certainty that their prayers will deliver them from evil. Meanwhile, others are feeling an anguish and sadness because of mankind's continued belief that God chooses sides. Yet, I still think there is hope. Despite the reality of war and the primitive instincts within us that allow for and even approve of war as a rational method of resolving conflict, my hope persists. I see it as more than wishful thinking, too. After all, there was a time when we thought the Iron Curtain was set for generations, that enmity between Ireland and England was forever, that Turks and Greeks inherited and nurtured a hatred that passed like a grotesque heritage from generation to generation, and that the hardness in the hearts of Indians and Pakistanis was destined to remain frozen in the mountains of Kashmir. All these testaments to stupidity and cruelty seem to be on the road toward resolution. Some day there will be peace in the Middle East. There is more than enough blame and recrimination to go around and around. But I believe, despite my unwarranted optimism, that a generation of Jews and Arabs will decide that it is time to live together in peace. It will indeed take more than wishful thinking to resolve the suffering and injustice that reign today, but we have a wealth of resources to address these challenges without recourse to military power.

Pacifism, particularly the Quaker variety, says that simply refusing to bear arms is not what it is all about. Nor is pacifism an act of cowardice where we choose to let others risk their lives in our defense. Pacifism does not embody an attitude of denigrating those who choose to participate in our armed forces. We don't point the finger of scorn at the soldier although we are profoundly saddened by what he has to do. Pacifism is really about creatively working for the removal of the causes of war. We try to appeal to the nobler instincts of adversarial leaders and alleviate the suffering and deprivation among all people and for whatever reasons that deny them at least some share of the good things in life. Is this the hopeless vision of a dreamer? I don't think so. We have not yet plumbed the depths of the human reservoir of kindness and our enormous capacity for caring, empathy, and the sharing of our resources.

Circles: Unity and Diversity

Almost any established house of worship, ranging from the huge and majestic cathedral to a simple Quaker meeting house, will have warm and cheerful volunteers or designated "greeters," whose pleasant task is to welcome attendees to their religious services. Some congregations will reach out into the community in an effort to bring new members into their distinctive circle. Some, like Jehovah's Witnesses and Mormons, will more aggressively reach out to your very door in an effort to bring you into the one and only circle ordained by God. And even in the ecumenical thrust toward the goal of merging, the separateness of the circles persists.

Then, like an ecclesiastical system of taxonomy that pays homage to the spirit of *apartheid,* we note the imposition of circles within circles—each circle defining the religious identity of the congregants. There are at least five different circles within the Jewish community, dozens of Protestant denominations, a multitude of Catholic orders, and other groupings keyed to global regions, nationality, and ethnicity. Sharply separated circles encompass the Sunni and Shiite distinctions in the Muslim world.

The apparently conflicting human inclinations of movement toward unity versus being supportive of continued diversity may need a new way of looking at it.

We could benefit from an unconventional view of an old, familiar enigma and see it differently—something like rotating a globe of the world so that our line of sight goes directly to the South Pole. The familiar equator isn't there and it all looks so strange until we remind ourselves that it's the same old world, but we're looking at it differently.

I see this experience as something analogous to a principle proposed by Niels Bohr as a consequence of his remarkable ability to resolve apparently contradictory scientific principles by looking at them from a radically different perspective. Early in the twentieth century, physicists argued about the nature of light—does it have a particle nature or is it a wave phenomenon? Both views seem to be amply supported by experimental verification—the photoelectric effect (photon-electron particle interaction) on one hand, and diffraction patterns (a characteristic of wave motion) on the other. Bohr's vision effectively replaced an *either-or* conflict with a *principle of complementarity*. He said, in effect, that the two very different descriptions of the nature of light taken together (complementarity), would give a more complete and accurate description of the phenomenon. Amazing what a different perspective, a fresh insight, an intuitive leap, or even a mystical revelation can do. Imagine any one of us holding the globe in an unusual way so that we see Tierra del Fuego instead of Paris or Istanbul. Despite some ongoing ridicule and rejection, Bohr's principle finally did resolve the problems dealing with wave-particle duality in a quantum mechanical description of electrons in atoms.

So, what is this vision I have in hope of resolving the unity-diversity dichotomy in religious experience? I doubt the originality of my vision, but what I see is a complementarity in which we benefit by always looking for

47

the more positive and constructive application. We can lean toward an emphasis on diversity when movement toward unification bogs down. We know this will happen. We have all seen how self-serving, nitpicking, adversarial attitudes can generate compromises that make everyone unhappy. And we have the frustrating, ponderous deliberations of committees or the Byzantine complexity of a worldwide hierarchy to give us second thoughts about the merits of unity. We wonder if an ecumenical tide toward unity can result in the fulfillment of the higher goals of organized religion. There is the shared monotheistic notion that since we all worship the same God, it gives us license to assume that we can now effectively alleviate worldwide suffering and misery. I don't believe this kind of unity will become a driving force toward the realization of a better life for more people—a quasi-utopian state, euphemistically called the *Peaceable Kingdom.*

Increasingly, I see the value of a kind of complementarity in the separate values of unity and diversity. Just as Bohr's principle allows us to describe light as photons or waves depending on which model that seems to more appropriate, we can similarly apply a principle of philosophical complementarity in choosing to go the route of unity or diversity. When diversity fragments into a kaleidoscopic chaos of bizarre cults—charismatic hate-mongers, faith healers, of flat-out con-artists to mention a few—the argument for consensus and unity becomes a more attractive focal point. We may even wonder about the essential truths and values of the various factions of mainstream religion—the levels of "orthodoxy," and the polar extremes separating Christianity's variety of churches and denominations. It's a most remarkable and somewhat disconcerting spectrum ranging from the extremes of the obscure little churches that feature mind control and weird rituals to aggressive evangelicals who will bring the "truth" to your door. And then it's on to divisions and subdivisions of mainstream Protestant churches and all the way through to the many orders of Eastern and Roman Catholicism.

Personally, I applaud variety in religious experience. The practically limitless number of identity circles provides each of us with a choice of the mode of worship and the sense of belonging that "speaks to our condition." It also provides a pathway to the inherent strengths of unity if we choose to draw, successively, the larger circle and then the even larger circle that will expand and enrich the dimensions of our identity.

While the complementing aspirations of unity and diversity properly rest on high moral ground, there is a caveat that begs for recognition. Simply, these noble goals are less than sacred. And why not? Even the principles by which we live are subject to modification and reordering with regard to priority. Clearly, this position has always caused absolutists to cringe. Anything that smacks of a "compromising of one's principles" is likely to be labeled "moral relativism" and regarded as an intolerably heretical walk out onto the worst of "slippery slopes." Any time-honored list of "Thou shalts" and "Thou shalt nots" will contain items that can be challenged in terms of relevance and value. The principles by which our ancestors lived, or for which they were prepared to die, may come across as mind-numbingly anachronistic today. When does the medieval concept of chivalry fit into any reasonable value system today? Who among us would agree to duel with pistols or swords in defense of someone's honor?

Today, a vast gray area in the unity-diversity arena involves affirmative action—a moral dilemma and a political football. Well-meaning, intelligent, and compassionate people advance convincing arguments for and against personnel selections that take into account and assign special value to race, ethnicity, gender, and age. These criteria are often granted significance equal to personality, intelligence, preparation, and proven performance. The motive force behind this movement toward racial balance may stem from a moral obligation to do the "right thing." It may derive from a sense of guilt or from a need to expiate the sins of past generations—or both. Regardless of the motive, or a complex bag of mixed motives, it is a noble endeavor to realize the beauty of diversity. Yet equally sincere and moral folk see the process as good-hearted but wrongheaded—a contravention of Martin Luther King's dream of a color-blind society. It has been characterized as a negation of the move toward the unity of mankind. More strongly, it is seen as reverse racism when selection is based on the color of one's skin. It may poison the outcome of a selection process by fostering a belief, or supporting an argument, that a less deserving candidate was picked because of a racially biased quota system. Trying to resolve questions like this will almost surely pull us out onto a superlubricated slippery slope. My gut feeling is that the question of affirmative action will fade into irrelevance in another generation or two. Overt segregation is largely gone. The dismantling of barriers to educational and job opportunities continues to give minorities a chance for a better life than menial servitude. With the continuing rise of an ethnically and racially expanded middle class, the justification of any kind of a quota system—regardless of how well-intentioned it may be—will become an interesting bit of modern history.

A contentious arena, in which I stand solidly on the side of diversity, is the increasingly expanding Western-world phenomenon of intermarriage. If this is perceived as a grand "melting pot" operation, the obvious question is how to make it work. Racial intermarriage is, paradoxically, both the easiest and most difficult to deal with. Easy, because there is no skin color compromise possible. The marital bond is the only unity since the changing of one's skin color is not an option. In a context of blunt clarity, a black and white couple cannot say, "Hey! Let's both of us be the same color." The hard part is in summoning up the will and determination to cope with the bigotry and insensitivity that still exist in our society. Cultural adjustments can be reconciled if there is a determination to discover and enjoy the richness of diversity.

Religious intermarriage is an altogether different animal. Unity is an option here. Many people assume that the most sensible course of action is for one partner to convert to the faith of the spouse. The choice of which way a conversion goes is a complex variable. It depends on external factors such as locale and the pressures of family and friends and the uniquely personal factors such as how strongly embedded are the beliefs, the visceral fears of the unknown, prejudices, and the indelible imprinting of childhood experiences linked powerfully to ritual, ceremony, and tradition.

The unity that conversion affords may be an easy way out. It's a way of avoiding potential conflicts such as which faith will form the religious identity of the children or what religious holidays will be celebrated. Clearly, conversion may involve great difficulties, too. It may amount to an insurmountable obstacle for many people steeped in the culture and religious traditions of their family. For them, conversion is a wrenching decision bordering on the unthinkable or even outrageous. There may be a sense of betrayal of the heritage entrusted to them by relatives and friends. The family attitudes and beliefs that become part of our core being as we grow up, as well as societal pressures, cannot be trivialized. Periodically, one reads newspaper and magazine accounts that catalogue and describe the apprehensions of "guardians of the faith" (i.e., people who vigorously oppose intermarriage) who fear the loss of congregants and the dilution and perversion of their religious traditions as a consequence of intermarriage conversions.

It brings me back to the analogy of circles again. The mixed religion marriage brings together two distinctly separate circles that stand as a contradiction to a conversion scenario that allows for only one. The resulting unity may require a great sacrifice of precious customs and traditions for one member of the couple. It may involve some spiritual pain for both—a loss of religious identity for one and a sense of guilt for the other, who may be overwhelmed by a vague sense of obligation to impose his or her religious convictions on the spouse. There seems to be a force operative here that is nonrational when normally respectful, sensitive, and caring people can brook no compromise or flexibility in matters of religious identity. The inability or unwillingness to accept an overlapping of the two circles, or the inclusive drawing of a larger circle that celebrates and incorporates the whole spectrum of religious affiliations, seems to me to be an abdication of the kind of respect that needs to be the foundation of a truly loving partnership. I don't see how people can truly love one another apart from an environment of mutual respect.

Respect, in the context of the mixed marriage, translates into a celebration of diversity. To me, this means a willingness to embrace joyfully the whole bag of traditions and holidays that are deeply ingrained in the lives of the husband and wife. It means the celebration of Christmas *and* Hanukkah or Kwanza or the winter solstice—decorating the tree and lighting the candles. It means heralding the arrival of springtime with the painting of Easter eggs as well as settling down to an ecumenical Passover seder. *Respect* is the casualty when we are "offended" by the inclusion of alien rituals or when a negative attitude of exclusivity wells up within us. Some people have convinced themselves that participation in the celebration of religious traditions other than their own somehow trivializes beliefs that are not mutually shared. I disagree strongly. To me, the universal celebration of the customs and traditions of others is a way of honoring "that of God" within them. I choose to dip my fingers into the holy water fonts of a Catholic church, to wear a skullcap and prayer shawl in a Hebrew temple, to be on my knees and touch my head to the rug in an Islamic mosque, to chant and spin the prayer wheel in a Buddhist temple, or to sit expectantly in the dynamic silence of a Quaker meeting.

I find in none of these experiences a betrayal of my own heritage. I see nothing trivial or insincere in my wish to respond to "that of God" in all people of all religions by participating with them in the observance of their sacred rites at their house of worship. Singing hymns or reciting words in a prayer book is important to me because I see such participation as a way of offering the gift of respect to those who believe in the beauty and sacredness of that mode of worship. I know well that my position is one that will earn the rebuke and anger of contrarians who are fixated on a curious sense of loyalty. Some will prefer to see participation in the rituals of others as an intrusion that they will find offensive. Again, I disagree strongly. I believe an extraordinary experience of the most beautiful kind of diversity is when we can get beyond the negativity of family and friends who misjudge our motives.

I think hypocrisy becomes a troubling reality only when there is intent to deceive ourselves and deliberately set out with sad intentions to deceive people whom we respect. Respect for "that of God" in humankind is the foundation and core of whatever my belief system may be. My relationship to God manifests itself in this way.

Drawing Bold Lines

Deciding where we stand on controversial issues is an ever challenging aspect of our human condition. Legal and biblical scholars will forever study and debate the centuries-old writings of sages and prophets whose lives had been dedicated to interpreting what are *truth, right action,* and *ethical behavior.* Revered writings such as the Bible, Koran, and our US Constitution are commonly regarded as nearly sacred items. Still, we are frustrated in our search for perfect guidance and infallibility when the search is restricted to "The Word" as the ultimate frame of reference. Polarizing debates about the justification of war, the morality of abortion, the legality of euthanasia, the ethical justification of embryonic stem cell research, and the separation of church and state, to mention a few, remain unresolved and without much likelihood of consensus. Given whatever principles by which we may choose to live, how do we decide which principle ranks above others in the context of our own personal value system? Eventually, deciding on which side of the fence we choose to plant our feet *vis-à-vis* an ethical or moral dilemma, we may have to summon the courage to walk out onto a slippery slope. Where absolutes confuse rather than clarify sticky issues, we have only our imperfect value system to help us decide where we draw the line. In the face of the inevitability of passionate adversarial arguments on the *pros* and *cons* in these polarizing debates, we will have to lay them out, superimpose our value system as a moral template, and then draw the line boldly.

For example, there is the commandment *Thou shalt not kill.* Implicit here is that life is sacred. *All* life? Does this mean no war, no abortion, no self-defense, no capital punishment, and no euthanasia? What about animals? Why is it that the killing of nasty life-forms like rats, poisonous snakes, parasitic insects, etc., is likely to earn approval while the killing of cute and cuddly furry animals is called barbaric? Where do we boldly draw a line if we choose not to die of starvation or pestilence?

A vegetarian draws a line between the animal and vegetable kingdoms. I once heard a vegan, in a fit of righteous indignation, describe a hamburger as a piece of charred, mutilated, dead cow. Okay . . . . In what I would call a mildly distorted perspective, he was using ugly, negative prose to inject a little dramatic shock value to his rhapsodizing about the beauty and sanctity of animal life. That's where he drew his line. Other people will tolerate the killing of a reptile while getting very upset about possibly harming a domesticated animal. So they've drawn their line.Shifting now from the relatively benign to the more seriously bizarre, wartime killing generates a chaos of bold lines for us. Considering concepts such as the *just war,* the *police action,* the *preemptive strike,* and ranging to the far side of the morality spectrum, we arrive at positions embodied in the *Quaker Peace Testimony.* The Quaker testimony against the bearing of arms, or the Gandhian total devotion to nonviolence, brings us to the point at which our unique value systems suggest where we draw our lines.

I find it untenable that in civilized societies, governmental agencies can legitimize and perform executions. Practical and moral arguments for and against notwithstanding, I am appalled that our revered justice system prates about the power of mercy, forgiveness, and redemption while permitting judges and juries to draw lines such that the execution of humans is sanctioned. What I find as even more incredible is that many of the righteous hypocrites who support capital punishment also support the violent acts of radical activists who will both assassinate doctors who perform abortions and destroy their clinics. I don't see an unborn fetus, before the first three or four months of gestation, as a conscious human being. That's where I boldly draw my line. Although abortion is usually a regrettable and rather extreme measure, the physical and mental well-being of the pregnant woman is the most important consideration. I agree, and so I boldly draw another line.

On the subject of nonviolence, we have other lines to draw, and I draw mine again. Not so boldly, however, because I have made some concessions to my human nature—rife with inconsistencies and character defects. Taking the Gandhian spirit to an extreme, I have met individuals who avowed that under no circumstances would they resort to violence. If they could not reason with a person who was about to assault them, they would stoically permit themselves to be sacrificed. Here I do draw a very firm line because I am not willing to sacrifice my life for an abstraction such as a creedal statement or for a geopolitical entity like my country. For the honor and advancement of such things, I prefer to live.

Martyrdom will never make it to the list of principles by which I live. I see elements of a grotesque oxymoron in that rejected proposal. To me, martyrdom is a cultural aberration and, philosophically, is a most disturbing contradiction of my most fundamental belief in the sacredness of humankind and the miracle of consciousness.

I have met absolute pacifists who have said they prefer the death of themselves and their loved ones rather than resort to violence by way of defense. I even knew a much-loved American disciple of nonviolence who seated himself in a public square, doused himself with gasoline, and lighted a match. His horrific act of self-immolation was his way of protesting the war in Vietnam. He was honored by some as a martyr. The line I drew placed him among the tragically misguided who died in vain for a cause that could have been better served by his living testimony.And now we have suicide bombers—the zealous fanatics who would be martyrs for God and for faithfulness to their bizarre interpretation of the Koranic command to defend the faith and destroy the infidels. I find myself shocked and outraged whenever people subscribe to the belief that it is laudable to die for a cause—honor, patriotism, church, political system, etc. I could certainly *risk* my life and well-being to save a family member or dear friend by donating part of a vital organ or whatever I have by way of material resources, but I could not offer my life as a sacrifice toward that end. There is, however, a huge difference between a willingness to risk one's life for a precious someone else and the purposeful laying down of one's life for the professed love for, or devotion to, an ideal. That's where I draw my line, and with that line I make no suggestion of a universal rightness. It is no more than a reflection of who I am. It is what I believe at this time and with no assurance that I have grasped some facet of eternal truth. Whatever slow and fitful gain in wisdom may accrue, my value system will remain in a state of flux.

From time to time, I will venture out, fall and get banged-up on that slippery slope. People will see more clearly than I how some of the bold lines I have drawn shift around like desert sands. Am I a *true* pacifist or a flip-flopping opportunist who will refuse to participate in wars that I judge to be immoral on one hand, and admit to the justification of an international police action to preserve the peace on the other hand? I mean a genuine police action, not a reprehensible euphemism for aggression. Common decency, at the least, calls out for resistance to genocide, terrorism, and slavery. Even the choice to go with a police action requires another walk out onto the slippery slope. Where in our value system do we find the principles that will yield the most effective and humane ways in which a police action can succeed? There is no simple answer, of course. Each conflict comes with its own unique set of causes and requires its own unique set of responses. We will, indeed, be caught up in inconsistencies despite attempts to apply universal formulas like rules of warfare and Geneva conventions. Consistency is hardly an absolute anyway. Remember, Oscar Wilde called consistency the last refuge of the unimaginative. Perhaps. A whimsical assessment, but I like it. War as a method of addressing any part of the spectrum of human disorders constructively is to me an anachronistic persistence of Dark Ages mentality. The primal instinct of self-preservation is within all of us, and that is good. But the horror of war leaves us traumatized when the realization of this instinct makes it necessary to depersonalize other human beings—to demonize and hate them and snuff out lives seen beyond the end of a rifle barrel or as nameless life-forms miles away from our own weapons of mass destruction. Again, there is a bold line waiting to be drawn.

Yes, I would register again as a conscientious objector, but never as an absolutist. I would have participated in World War II in some way short of bearing arms, although I would have respected those who chose or were assigned combatant status. For me, it's not an inner compulsion to hunger and thirst after righteousness. It is, rather, a stumbling, lurching movement in the evolution of my identity. My definition of pacifism is described by a life that respects and cherishes "that of God" in everyone so that it effectively takes away the occasion for war.

TheMind-Body Interface

This seems like a good time to recognize the obvious fact that my mind needs to stop taking itself too seriously—to come back into my body, which is where it lives (if I'm allowed a rash assumption); to slither back into the cranial mush between my ears. There are few rare individuals like the British astrophysicist Stephen Hawking, whose paralyzed body is still able to accommodate a genius mentality. A guy like me has to find ways to maintain a reasonably fit body so that my mind, with all its faults and foibles, can do its job without causing too much embarrassment.Mind and brain—which compose the essential center of human consciousness, are commonly regarded as two synonymous words, but they are not quite the same thing. Instead of an unnecessarily lengthy technical effort to explain what I mean, I'll use an example to make an admittedly silly distinction. Here goes: our little cat, Roger, has an amazing brain. He can leap tall cabinets in a single bound; he can walk the narrowest ledge without fear of falling. If my brain could have allowed me the same comparably exquisite eye-muscle coordination and leaping ability as our cat, I might have been a great athlete. But, obviously, that's not the way it works. While the physical powers of our cat's *brain* may amaze me as I observe the things he can do, there's not much of a *mind* to allow for serious reasoning. Oh, I suppose he has enough mind in that little brain so that he will express love for an affectionate owner. Rejoice, people! We've got mind and brain together even though we don't know where and how they merge to become what I call the miracle of human consciousness.Clearly, then, if we are to experience the fullness of life, we must pay attention to the wellness of our bodies—without a live and active brain there can be no mind function. Proper diet and exercise for the care of the body and the brain is what it's all about. Sure, we know that because all forms of communication media beat us over the head with the message every day. Since there's not too much mystery about what constitutes a sensible diet, I'll focus on exercise here because I have a drum to beat. I'm partial. I have favorites like hiking and running. I know these are not options for everyone. There are many among us who would love to run but have cardiac issues, bad knees, back pains, etc. Of course there is golf, tennis, swimming, skiing, and so on as wonderful alternatives.Running is my thing, and I want to tell you why. And it's not the competitive aspect that I'll be pushing. For me, running is about fun and fitness. Fitness is what we have with a well-functioning cardiovascular system. Our endurance holds up, and we can run mile after mile without feeling faint or weary. Layers of belly flab melt away. Muscle tone increases noticeably. Sometimes, if we persevere and are a little lucky, we may even experience the fabled "runner's high." This is what can happen when the body produces a chemical group of secretions called endorphins that can transport us into a state of euphoria. It is the great exertion of a long run that gives us an absolutely euphoric feeling of being above and beyond the physical stress of pain and exhaustion. It's kind of a fulfillment of unspoken yearnings—a triumph over the burden of limitations that we tend to put upon ourselves. We don't have to beat any other person to the finish line. It's enough to simply vanquish our own inner doubts.

The running I love the most is that which takes me through woodland trails and all kinds of challenging terrain. I love solo runs, where there are only the sights and sounds of nature. I also enjoy the alternative activity of running with friends. This provides much wonderful social interaction, and with it comes the fun part. I'll say it again: it's all about fun and fitness. Competition is a part of the worldwide running scene, and it will always be a matter of choice. Many people thrive on competition to the extent that games and teams and winning are all that matter. During the years that I was running races on tracks, from five kilometres to marathons, I met people whose all-consuming purpose was to win a medal or trophy. I've been there and done that, as we say, but it's so sad when that becomes the whole point of competing. I respect their right to be that way, but I totally disagree.

Fun, fitness, and a negative attitude toward competitive obsession will be my segue into an introduction of a worldwide running movement that is bizarre, unconventional to the extreme, and probably a little insane. I run with one of these groups I'm about to describe. We're known as Hash House Harriers. With "hashers," as we're called, it's all about fun and fitness—even though our brains are a bit defective, and our minds are twisted. Before continuing, however, I should make an effort to allay some possible feelings of shock and raised eyebrows because of the word "hash." It has absolutely nothing to do with the narcotic *hashish*. Nothing at all! I mention it because people do jump to wrong conclusions sometimes, especially when the word is used by a disreputable-looking bunch of trail runners. I had such an experience just a few years ago when I joined an expedition of runners in Peru. We were there to run the Inca Trail to Machu Picchu on our way to a mountain circuit high in the Andean mountains. Our group decided to visit a popular bar in the city of Cusco before starting the run, and it was there that we met a crowd of young women from Holland. Since my son and his family live in Amsterdam, I cheerfully approached their table in a smiling fit of cordiality and pointed to my sweatshirt emblazoned with the words, *Amsterdam House Hash Harriers.* My expectation of an appreciative response, perhaps with a huzzah or two thrown in, was instead met with facial expressions somewhere between blank and incredulous. Then, one of their group came right out and asked me why I had come all the way to Peru to sell hash. My effort to explain what the word "hash" on my sweatshirt meant and to explain that I belonged to a running group called Hash House Harriers, failed. They were sure I was an old dope dealer who ought to be ashamed of himself. I can visualize their smirky comments to friends back in Holland when they told the story of this sleazy American liar who was selling dope to young adventurers.Let me give you a thumbnail description of how all this craziness started. I don't know how or when it will end, but that's beside the point. Okay . . . . here we go. Sometime around 1937 a bunch of English soldiers were doing their bit to support an outpost of the British Empire in the Malaysian city of Kuala Lumpur. Not only were these guys bored and homesick, but they were quite unhappy with the terribly uninspired food served in the mess hall—which they called a "hash house." This same name was applied to the few and far between pubs run by British expats. And so, like a beautiful flower rising up out of the muck, a brilliant idea was born as an escape from the dull routine of daily life.

It all goes back to a game invented by kids at the Rugby School in England about a century before the Kuala Lumpur debacle. The game was called "hounds and hares," and it worked by designating some of the boys as hares. The hares would proceed to lay a trail of paper bits over a terrain of hedges, bogs, streams, and hills ahead of the other boys, the hounds, whose job it was to catch them (and probably subject them to whatever indignities that might enter their sadistic little minds). This was a mild variation of the schoolboy game the soldiers decided to play. The terrain now was the whole jungle surrounding Kuala Lumpur. The possibilities of getting lost, eaten by tigers, or being captured by rebels added a whole new dimension. The rules were simple enough—designated hares laid the paper trail from one pub to another. Since the pub was just another hash house (fortunately able to supply warm beer) and the players were cross-country runners, known as harriers, the grand name applied to this bunch was "Hash House Harriers." With the passing of time, the bizarre game caught on and spread throughout the world. There are about 2000 hashes (or kennels) in more than 180 countries. I belong to one, and now I'll tell you something about being a Hash House Harrier. I call it:

The Mystique of the Hash House Harriers

What is it about hashing that casts its spell over us and feeds our addiction? Hashing is, after all, a weird aberration in the world of recreational running. I raise the question, rhetorically, because curious people ask about it. They don't understand what it is that makes mature adults participate in an activity where the downsides and hazards seem so obvious. They wonder why we seem to abuse our bodies and risk our necks by running through inhospitable terrain—thickets clogged with thorns poised to shred the skin of our legs, and venues burgeoning with poison ivy, ticks, bees, and whatever creepy-crawly thing that may be endemic to a particular corner of the world. Why do we choose to run up and down slippery trails filled with rocks and roots? What reckless impulse drives the hares to lay trails that make us climb over and through cyclone fences and barbed wire, and slosh through streams and swampland rich in sneaker-sucking mud? What defects in our collective character allow us to trespass on farmland, private estates, and golf courses, or cause security guards to get incredibly apprehensive when we saunter through shopping malls?

Why do we court disaster by feeling our way through dark, water-filled culverts and tootling along stretches of railroad tracks? People wonder how men and women—especially men—can reconcile themselves to a degree of shamelessness that goads them into participating in a huge slice of lunacy called a "Red Dress Run." Who were the warped minds that conjured up an event in which free spirits reign supreme and the masses, garishly decked out in red dresses, career around crowded business districts in cities throughout the world while yelling inanities like, "On, on!" or just screeching like banshees. And if we're really lucky, all this neat stuff might go on during a thunderstorm, a blizzard, or in the dark of night.

Our favored response is to tell perplexed mortals, "We're a drinking club with a running problem!" We think it's a pretty cute rejoinder, and it often brings about a broad smile and maybe a shout of approval . . . . but it's also misleading, and it doesn't always turn out to be the perfect little snappy remark we want it to be. To some onlookers it is a validation of their moral indignation. They feel there's something scandalous about this kind of bizarre behavior being displayed by a bunch of freaky people—people so deficient in basic "family values" that they let themselves get caught up in a wave of mob psychology that makes it okay to be seen as offensive or infantile. The misleading part is the inherent suggestion that hashers are a bunch of boozers. Not so! Emphatically, not so! One of the wonderful things about most hashers is their unstated and unspoken resolve to never put pressure on anyone to use alcoholic beverages. It is clearly understood that some people prefer not to use alcohol. They just don't like it, or health considerations rule it out. These hashers are accorded total respect. We don't even joke about it.

Sometimes our response to anal-retentive mentalities derives from an oft-stated conviction that says, "If you're talking to a hasher, you *don't need* to explain your addiction. If it's not a hasher, you *can't* explain it." I don't think so. We may find easy comfort in this answer, but it's a little too trite and too smug. It's a cop-out. I think we can give people answers that will make more sense. Some of them might even decide to give hashing a try. Here, then, is one hasher's attempt to describe what this is all about. There's no rationale for the order of topics as presented. There's no progression from trivial to powerful—just a bunch of reasons in support of the Hash House Harrier mystique.

It's not enough to say that it's just about fun and fitness. A lot of running clubs feature that slogan, and, in a sense, it says it all. It becomes an important statement to the effect that our passion is not necessarily related to competition, winning, or ego inflation. Paradoxically, however, it says nothing at all until we get into some details to explain what we mean by "fun" and how we experience a *joie de vivre* that you just can't get with treadmills and barbells. Oh yes, the fitness gym has its place, and I'll head for one three days a week for a sweat and strain routine. While the "no pain, no gain" approach is not exactly fun, it does work, and it requires no justification. It is a solid contribution to our fitness. Hashing, by contrast, is an alternative to the world of grunting, stinking, sweating bodies holed up in a jungle of steel contraptions. Hashing leads to a different level of fitness that contributes to soundness of body in a less aggressive way.

Men and women of all ages regularly savor the joy of a group activity that takes us bounding over trails through forests, along (and often into) ponds and rivers, over high meadows, and even over patches of asphalt.

The variety of locales is wonderful, too. Hardly ever do we run the same trails we've run before in familiar places. The noncompetitive aspect of hashing is a joyous release from the oval track, stop watches, and finishing chutes of the good old 10 K road race. Of course we find fun and camaraderie at the road races, too. Lots of hashers are also avid competitors—it doesn't have to be an either/or choice. When they've paid the entrance fee and pinned a numbered bib to their shirts, many of them want to win their share of medals and trophies (to go along with yet another T-shirt). There may be an added good feeling when the runners know that a significant portion of the money involved goes to a worthwhile charity or fund for things like cancer research. Let's not fail to recognize, also, the huge sense of accomplishment that comes when a first-time marathoner manages to cover the whole twenty-six miles.

The hash rewards, however, include a higher level of camaraderie that can only exist among close friends—mutually shared expressions of warmth and affection doled out with hugs and smiles that extend naturally beyond the hash event. We enjoy getting together for nonrunning social events, too. Periodically, hashers will gather for a trip to the seashore or mountains, a dinner at an exotic restaurant, a special big event like a ballgame or concert, or maybe just meeting together for a happy hour at a local brewpub to celebrate someone's birthday. We don't feature prizes and awards at our activities other than a mug of beer or two for anyone who's silly enough to think they won something. Toward that end, we bring a characteristically perverse humor by presenting "down-down" awards (i.e., mugs of beer) to the hares for grossly mismanaging the whole event, lazy shortcutters, speedy front-runners, shocked visitors who had no idea of what they were getting into, and new hashers (referred to as "cherries," "virgins," or "new boots"). The "award ceremony" is like nothing else. With the flimsiest and totally unsupported accusations, we proceed to reward the cheaters and punish the hares and all the others. The eating and drinking climax to our physical exertions is called an "apres," in which our elected "religious advisor," striving for a high level of refreshing irreverence, leads us in the singing of appropriately raunchy tunes.

The variety of personalities that you're likely to find in a typical local hash is quite amazing. And it's not only the individual hashers—the hash as an entity is likely to have a personality. Some like to run, while others prefer to party. We've got the potty-mouth crowd on one hand and just a few goody-two-shoes evangelicals on the other. In a light-hearted way, the hash disdain for "gung ho" runners makes them use the word "run" as though it was an obscenity. They're also quick to ridicule any hashers who dare to wear T-shirts from road races. Such heresies will surely earn them a "down-down" at the apres. Other hashes are infested with a few serious runners who thirst after physically daunting trails. They may even manage to create a kind of competitive twist to the event. Apparently, the primal forces of our human nature will cause the competitive fire to burn in contradiction of the hash mentality. And then, some hashers love to sing—the raunchier the lyrics, the better. Most hashes, however, embrace the whole spectrum of motivations.

But back to the individual, because here is where we have something special in the social interactions of all kinds of men and women hashers. What is wonderful about it, and what is something of a unique hash phenomenon, is the total, unquestioning acceptance that hashers have for each other. People do not come to the hash with agendas that include a need to impress others with how important, or rich, or how smart they are. Nobody cares if you're a plumber, stockbroker, big-shot executive, tax collector (well, that might create some negative disposition), lawyer (with a high tolerance for nasty jokes), chemistry professors like me (the worst kind), or whatever. Criteria for acceptance into hash events are simply a few bucks to pay for food and drink, a love of adventure running on trails, and a zest for partying that is likely to be on the "R-rated" side.

With regard to attitudes and philosophies, the hash is typically a place of diversity: conservatives and liberals, religious types, irreverent characters, party animals as well as quiet loners, and some people that drift in who are right off the wall. But these unique personalities are warmly welcomed, and we don't call them weird. We prefer to say they are just different, and the encompassing arms of the hash are long enough and strong enough to encircle them all. One of the really delightful things about hashing is the chance we have to react to the smothering effect of political and social "correctness."—to be a rebel. To leave, temporarily, our sheltered structures and directed workaday worlds that are so filled with expectations and responsibilities. There are no *rules* in the hash universe. The hash is the time and place for behavior based on a mock disrespect for genteel conventions. But it's done in a spirit of fun, and that's why it exists and works as a major part of the hash mystique. There's a lot of tongue-in-cheek insulting that goes on, a kind of crude banter that causes smiles rather than hurt feelings. It is clearly understood that teasing is just a light-hearted bit of fluff among people who have profound respect and genuine affection for each other. It's the hash style to kid people about mismanaging events, laying ugly trails, or botching up whatever it is that somebody with a brain (or, half a mind) would do correctly

Another unique characteristic of the worldwide hash movement is the special nickname that assembled hashers hang on a newly inducted member. The age, gender, or lifestyle of the newcomer is irrelevant. The envelope-pushing approach is basic to any flimsy pretext for selecting a raunchy name for the victim about to undergo a beer baptism. No examples here, but I'll note that this singular event allows the hash to cross the line separating decency from the realm of poor taste and cruelty toward wildlife (i.e., hashers).

Of course, the world of the hash has its share of human imperfection. Most of us will have that kind of day where we feel a little grouchy and behave in a way that rubs somebody's fur the wrong way. Where you draw the line between good-natured taunting and overly crude insults varies with people. Some folks can handle an unrestricted litany of jokes and songs and always find the humor. But when you get into jokes involving sexual orientation, toilet functions, race, ethnicity, blondes, and lawyers, some people will feel deeply offended. What distinguishes "humor" from bad taste and gross insensitivity will always be perceived differently by different people. Personality clashes are another inevitability, but that's something we all have to learn to live with. What is great about the hash is the degree of harmony that seems to have become one of the major characteristics of our remarkably inclusive society.

It is largely because of this spirit, this attitude, that the hash movement has evolved into an unstructured, but nevertheless international, affiliation. For example, it is absolutely fantastic how a hasher from one part of the world can get on the Internet and hit on the web pages of hashers thousands of miles away, and then, choosing among the e-mail addresses displayed, contact an officer of any foreign hash, introduce yourself, and announce that you plan to be there on such and such dates. And then you may ask about any hasher who might have enough room for you to crash during your brief stay. Look for a positive response. There is a real sense of fraternity among hashers throughout the world that opens doors and multiplies friendships.

Another Kind of Circle

In my earlier essay, called "A Perspective on Circles," I used the imagery of large and small circles as a way of getting into the questions of inclusion and exclusion. I'm using a different property of a circle here to grapple with a problem I suggested earlier. It's a question that has tormented humankind since the evolution of consciousness: *Why do bad things happen to good people?* If there is a loving God, in whose image we are supposed to have been made, we are driven to ask why he/she so often seems to trash our standard concepts of justice and fair play. Why are the innocent, righteous, and defenseless among us subjected to suffering and deprivation? The question why is the starting point on this circle . . . . and that's the problem because this circle has no definitive starting point. And it has no ending point we can label as a satisfactory "Because." It begins with a why and comes back to the same why . . . . again and again—leaving us distraught and perhaps bitter if we believe we are among the good people who don't deserve whatever mode of suffering that leaves, or has left, our lives stripped of joy and hope.

Now, instead of continuing in this vein of morbid generalization, I will try to deal with this question of *why* as it was asked by our daughter, Lise, before she died from the accumulated ravages of cerebral palsy in the year 2000, at the age of thirty-eight. It's more than ten years ago now, but it's something one never really "gets over." There are some powerfully mixed feelings that we have to deal with—a reconciliation of extreme opposites: our loss of a beloved daughter *vis-à-vis* her freedom from pain and suffering. We had to find the perspective that could let us deal with the selfishness of wanting to keep her alive forever instead of rejoicing in the fact that we had her with us for more joyful years than anyone gave us reason to hope for. We had to gratefully and graciously accept the essential reality that Lise's vibrant life had run its course. It was time for us to just let go and leave ourselves with the vision of her sleeping peacefully with her arm around the stuffed Siberian tiger she loved to hold.

Finally, it was an end to the interminable regimen of drugs that ultimately wrecked the functioning of her internal organ system. And most amazing, to the point of being almost miraculous, was the warmth and joy she shared with everyone despite the frustration of being locked within a body that made it so difficult to verbally express her thoughts and feelings. No longer did she have to deal with muscles that had a mind of their own. This final sleep banished the physical torment and removed forever the never ending round of hospital stays and operations. In addition to an amazingly happy disposition that simply radiated from her in spite of the crushing weight of her disabilities, Lise had a remarkable zest for life. She had a wonderful sense of humor to go with everything else, and it was startlingly sophisticated, too. She loved wordplay with puns and double entendres, and she'd laugh uproariously at language gaffes.

In a more serious vein, and more to the point of these meditative recollections, I want to write about a topic that was one of the heavier philosophical questions that Lise and I talked about from time to time. Regarding her cerebral palsy affliction and its attendant store of unremitting pain and endless list of handicaps, Lise sometimes verbalized, slowly and painstakingly, the question, "Why me?" As her designated fountain of wisdom, I was supposed to have the answer. Of course, it couldn't be the answer she might have been hoping for because I didn't have it. She wanted to believe there was some sense to all this—some meaning and maybe hope that somewhere down the road a cure might be about to emerge. We labored with questions like this, and for me it was a revelation of a depth of intelligence in our daughter that is not easily seen. I was often delighted to answer Lise's questions about human biology or electrical circuits and things like that. She had an insatiable curiosity about our physical world, along with a capacity for wide-eyed astonishment that made it so much fun to talk with her about natural phenomena. I'm sure that some of my explanations would have horrified the experts, but they sat well with Lise. Her great speech impediment was interpreted by some as retardation because they often couldn't make sense out of what she was trying to say. How wrong they were! We could always peer into the depth of her eyes and commune with her and be bathed in the radiance of her smile. Lise had an incredibly warm personality and, always, that slightly offbeat sense of humor that was uniquely hers. One of the extraordinarily beautiful facets of Lise's personality was illustrated by the very effective way she had cultivated to deal with grievances, slights, petty cruelties and callousness brought about by the ignorance and insensitivity of some people. Somehow, Lise understood that people often meant well, but they simply didn't know how to relate to her. There's some powerful irony here when you think that Lise, who was dealt some bad cards in the "game of life," was able to savor the joy of living more fully than millions of people who had no physical handicaps like hers. I reminded her of that as I told her that it's not so much a matter of what cards have been dealt to you as it is the question of how you play the cards. A bit trite, admittedly, but powerful truisms tend to gain that status.

But this kind of speculation doesn't really come to grips with Lise's question of, "Why me?" We read and talked about a number of inspirational stories and biographies of people who have had lives filled with challenges similar to Lise's. The common redemptive theme was one of faith—a firm belief that whatever the nature of their misfortune, it was God's will. We all know how routinely people describe any natural disaster, such as floods, earthquakes, hurricanes and the like, as "an act of God." I suppose it may help to get insurance companies off the hook, but I prefer to see these disasters as natural chance rather than a purposeful act of a divine being. People will always believe that there must be some reason for their suffering, and God chose them to fulfill an incomprehensible purpose. That is a kind of blind faith that will always be supremely meaningful to many, but not to Lise. It didn't come close to answering her question, "Why me?" So, if blaming a capricious God doesn't work, where do we go from there? My movement was toward science. Not science for answers, but for the philosophy of science: uncertainty, tentativeness, discovery, and an attitude of genuine humility. What I said to Lise might be called a "cop-out," but it wasn't that because what I said was, "You're asking a question that we shouldn't ask." There is no answer that can relieve the torment and frustration of our having minds that cannot begin to fathom the notion that there might be some purpose to it all. To believe in suffering as a purposeful act of God requires an absolutely irrational leap of faith. My leaning will always be toward uncertainty and chance instead. The bad cards dealt to our daughter came out that way because of the random shuffle of the deck. What is *done* with the hand dealt to her finally gets to the operation of purpose. Instead us cursing our bad luck, we should more usefully focus on the miracles that fill our lives with joy. This is not a matter we can simply analyze and explain, because its nature lies in the basic mystery of brain-mind-soul interaction. We grasp some meaning, intuitively, but we don't really understand.

Let me address this concept of miracle by looking at a single phenomenon—a precious segment of reality—which is a smile. We walked into Lise's room, and, as our eyes met, the sequence of events began. All the reflected light enters the pupils of our eyes as trillions of light particles, or photons, per second. These photons continue through the lens of each eye and the thick fluid in the eyeball until it hits the retina and its hundred million rod and cone cells. The intensity of the light hitting the retina varies with the reflected highlights and shadows caused by us and the objects in the room. And the scenery is changing microsecond by microsecond and recorded in perfect, seamless detail. Our glistening lips make the corners of the retinas experience a blast of high intensity at the very instant other corners are slightly jogged by a few photons that make their way from the folds and shadows that compose our images.

Each one of the trillions of photons comes to rest as it is absorbed by a retinine molecule. In darkness, the retinine molecule, made of twenty carbon atoms, twenty-eight hydrogen atoms, and an oxygen atom, is attached to a protein molecule and has a twist in its "backbone" of carbon atoms. The incoming light affects the structure so that trillions of retinine molecules are untwisted and separated from the protein every second. This goes on—second by second by second. A few steps follow before the retinine molecule twists again and waits for the next photon—all of this happening in a tiny fraction of a moment since we first looked at each other.

Triggered by the dance of the retinine molecules, the nerve cells (neurons) change shape to block the flow of sodium ions in the surrounding salty body fluid. This blockage increases the voltage that powers electricity through the neuron until it goes about a hundred thousandth of an inch to pass the news to the next neuron. In another instant, the electrical signals reach a clot of neurons, called a ganglion, which we have in our optic nerves behind the eyes. Then the electrical message races to the brain for processing in a region known as the visual cortex. This is a small region of the brain made up of millions of neurons arranged in six layers of folded brain tissue. This is where the preliminary analysis starts and lasts for the duration of the time that our eyes are taking in the view.

And then, just think—if a sound is uttered, the miracle of hearing gets under way. With the certainty of an embrace, the miracle of touch sweeps over us. This just staggers our capacity for astonishment! We realize, at least in part, that we can come up with detailed explanations of these aspects of biological activity. And our partial understanding of what happens does nothing to diminish the grandness of the events. The even greater miracle of human consciousness is what we don't know very well at all. And again, there is the question why. Why does the meeting of our eyes cause the glory of a smile? Why do our smiles kindle a palpable glow of warmth and affection? Why does the miracle of the smile engulf us in absolute love? There are no answers to these whys. They don't need justification or analysis. They simply are. And they are there for us to savor and celebrate as the *truly* miraculous.

Our private grief is tempered by the certainty of Lise being forever alive in our hearts and thoughts. There is also a sense of her free spirit being with us as a mystical presence. Not in the form of a hovering ghost or an angel "up there," but a *reality* that is with us. In the metaphysical world of faith, philosophy, and dreams, sages have assured us that we can and do create our own realities. For us, the bold line that separates the tangible world of our senses from the realities we have created is blurred by the power of our emotions.

When Lise died in our arms it was the most dreadful reality of our lives. She is with us now—another kind of reality, however, filled with smiles, laughter, flush with the pastel paints she chose to use for her artwork, cluttered with her stuffed animals, and with all her family and friends who meant so much to her . . . and loved her in return.

Guiding Principles

Like any sojourner happily lurching and shuffling through life in search of purpose and meaning, I look for landmarks and road signs. I'll call these directions *principles by which to live*. It's hardly a God-given list of *do's* and *don'ts* in the form of admonitions and commandments. These principles are meant to stand as points of reference that might give me the best ways to deal with ethical dilemmas where shades of gray are more abundant than glossy contrasts of black and white.

Modern times have created a climate where professional ethicists are springing up like weeds. Universities have granted them endowed chairs and the authority to pontificate on right and wrong in human attitudes and behavior. These ethicists are a mixed bag—the moral absolutists who see everything in black or white on one side, and the gray-tone proponents of "situational ethics" on the other. Their arguments pound us incessantly. Almost daily, we read about their pronouncements in various printed media and via TV and radio as they sound off on topics like: When is bluntly stated opinion a matter of free speech instead of slander and libel? When should a fetus be characterized as a viable human infant as opposed to a mass of developing cells? At what point is written work freely available in the "public domain" and when do we cross the line into plagiarism and cheating? Can we proceed with cloning and embryonic stem cell research without usurping the prerogative of God? Can we justify the application of situational ethics when it may be more constructive and humane to "bend" the truth, destroy higher life-forms, do whatever it takes to ignore stupid and anachronistic laws so that the basic necessities of life—food, shelter, medicine, etc.—are provided for the poorest among us? Or do we prefer to simply criminalize these actions by just labeling them as lying, murder, and law-breaking?I don't have the answers. Any pretense in that direction would have to be incredibly arrogant. I'm not sure what constitutes the credentials of a universally accepted ethicist, but I know I don't have them. Like any mortal, struggling to do the best with what he has, I have my own variable, deeply flawed, and certainly inconsistent value system that I can partially set forth as a list of principles—a list that will always be in a state of hierarchical flux so that yesterday's top-ranked principle may be one of lesser rank today, depending on the situation at hand. Oh, yeah! I thrive out there on the slippery slope.So, without the benefit of a scary voice coming out of a burning bush or a weighty prophet coming down a mountain with a list of do's and don'ts carved into stone tablets, I'll list some of the principles by which I try to live. Give me a break! I *do* try . . . . most of the time.

1. Respect
This is usually number one. It derives from my belief that there is "that of God" in everyone. Without respect, I don't see how it's possible to love someone, even in the case of an intimate person to person interaction. Declaring a love for a person whom you can't respect seems to me to

be a contradiction of oxymoronic proportions. I choose to offer respect as a gift. No strings attached. No expectations of reciprocation. My respect only needs to be *earned* if someone has behaved in a way in which that gift has been abused. Although my main concern for the concept of respect is people oriented, it takes other forms, too. For animals, respect becomes meaningful when there is humane treatment—even for beasts of burden and those that end up on our dinner plates. For pets, there is the added layer of affection.

Respect is also a gift to Mother Nature. This is all about our stewardship for planet Earth, our only home in the universe. It means our whole-hearted efforts to preserve the environment: to collect and recycle the products of our natural resources we are working to conserve, to do whatever it takes to slow down global warming, to act against pollution of all kinds, to preserve and nurture our open spaces and wilderness areas, and to work against the irresponsible extinction of threatened species of animals and plants.

Respect is not to be confused with simple obedience or the bootlicking adoration of the powerful. It is not merely the handing out of praise and approval. True respect has its meaning in the genuine recognition of human dignity, the sacredness of life, and the miracle of consciousness.

A deeply ingrained commitment to respect the infinite value of all people can save us from becoming obsessed with the biblical hungering and thirsting after righteousness. Even the most saintly people throughout history have described the torment of "scrupulosity." They defined scrupulosity as an excessive concern for the living of life according to the absolute principles they accepted as the unambiguous will of God. I don't buy that. I refuse to be tormented by scruples, and I doubt seriously that I can know the will of God with any certainty. Total obsession with philosophical and theological absolutes is a kind of a parallel to a perfectionist attitude. Both have the common effect of paralyzing hopes and actions because of the fear that something might be lacking or that we might just be wrong.

My deep concern for a respectful interaction among people does not really come from a compulsion to conform to what I think is the will of God. I'm not sure that I will ever know with certainty what the will of God is. It's an attitude or a belief that seems to conjure up a relationship to a kind of an anthropomorphic, biblical vision of God—a model that does not speak to my condition. It is in the face of humankind that I find the face of the indescribable creator, and, hence, relationships short of genuine respect are nonsensical to me.

2. Love

Like the man says, " . . . . there is faith, hope, and love. And the greatest of these is love." As topics go, this is huge. It's bigger than huge, and the number of subtopics is practically endless. There are so many kinds of love, and so many forms in which it is realized. Here, in my list of principles (all two of them), I must necessarily focus on the kind of love that is personal—not an abstraction in which I talk about a love for humanity, or the world, or the scenic beauty of a sunset. For me, it's about the love I have for close family members and dear friends. It is an irrational, deeply emotional attachment to and involvement in their lives. It gives rise to enduring friendships that I eagerly cherish. It comes with an enduring ability to withstand the occasional stress and strain that comes with perceived slights, hurt feelings, misunderstandings, insensitivity, and the like. There is a way of dealing with a soul that may too easily get chafed and become raw. It's called "keeping things in perspective." There's a saying "out there" that suggests, *Don't sweat the small stuff.* I like that. I could almost rate it as principle number three, oozing such sagacity and wisdom as it does. There are so many components of love, even with a focus on the nature of the love shared among the closest of people—those within the smallest circle. It involves caring and relating seriously to their hopes and aspirations. It's about sometimes providing a strong back to help carry their burdens of responsibility. And always . . . . *always* to be there for them with an unlimited ration of warmth and affection. For me, love is a kind of holistic phenomenon that we give and receive spiritually *and* physically. The wholeness of its expression is realized in the heart and mind, in the voice and the gaze, and in the special warmth of a hug and a kiss.

A whole list of prioritized principles seemed to be the way to go when I started, but respect and love just seem to say it about right.

Stan Cherim was a professor of Physical Chemistry and researcher in Biophysics at the University of Pennsylvania. He resides with his wife, Solveig, in Wallingford, Pennsylvania. They were married in Denmark and proceeded to Tarsus, Turkey where Stan taught Science and Mathematics at the American College.

Stan and Solveig had two children, a son, Jan Gregersen, an international banking consultant, who lives with his family in the Netherlands. A daughter, Lise, who died in the year 2000, is featured in one of the essays in this book. She was a handicapped artist.

Stan received his undergraduate and graduate degrees in Biochemistry from the University of Pennsylvania. During his undergraduate years he was active in Track and Field, sang with the Men's Glee Club and Choral Society, and was the Quaker officer in the Christian Association. For several years he was involved in basic research in Cellular Respiration at the university's Johnson Foundation for Biophysics and Physical Biochemistry. Post graduate study followed at Cal Tech (Pasadena, CA), the Fermi Center for High Energy Particle Physics (Chicago,IL), the University of Copenhagen, and the Laboratory for Research in the Structure of Matter at Penn.

Currently, Stan remains active as a writer, a trail runner and trekker, and an adventure traveler. He remains active in the affairs of his Quaker Meeting.